About the Book

Abe Lincoln wasn't eager to begin his first day of school. He wasn't used to being among strangers, and he was afraid that the other students would laugh at his awkward new clothes.

In Kentucky he would attend the ABC, or "blab," school run by Zachariah Riney and the home-based school of "Indian lover" Caleb Hazel (where Abe earned the nickname Big Buck of the Lick). In Illinois the teachers Mentor Graham and Azel W. Dorsey had much influence on him. Each of these men was, to a different degree, committed to ideals of civil liberty.

But much that Lincoln learned came from the lonely wilderness environment. It was a world filled with superstitions and strange omens, grounded in a firm belief in God's will, a world of few books and newspapers, where a pioneer child "learned to listen, and listened to learn."

In this extensively researched historical biography, William H. Armstrong re-creates the rhythms and sayings of Lincoln's world with remarkable feeling and accuracy. Vivid descriptions of the teaching methods in the one-room schools, discussion of the straightforward ideas set forth in the books available to Lincoln and of the predominant beliefs of the time, offer an unusual, in-depth picture of the period, as well as valuable insights into Abraham Lincoln's character.

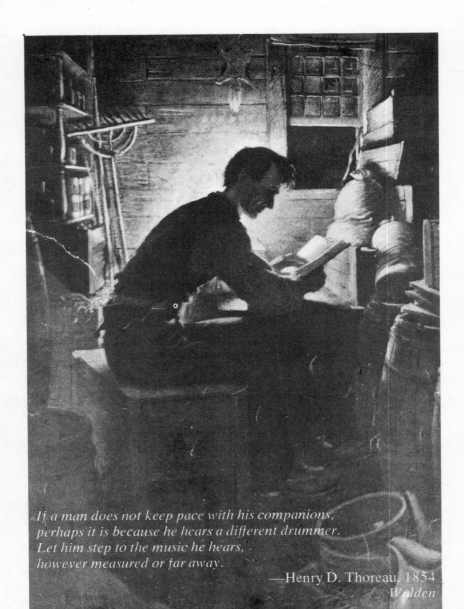

If a man does not keep pace with his companions,
perhaps it is because he hears a different drummer.
Let him step to the music he hears,
however measured or far away.

—Henry D. Thoreau, 1854
Walden

The Education of ABRAHAM LINCOLN

by William H. Armstrong

Coward, McCann & Geoghegan, Inc.

New York

The pictures are provided courtesy of:

Chicago & Illinois Midland Railway Co.   101

Illinois State Historical Society   113

Library of Congress   41, 85, 120

Lincoln National Life Foundation   21, 25, 27, 34, 51, 96

Museum of Natural History, Le Havre   62

New York Public Library   2, 8, 22, 80, 83, 88, 103, 118

John Ranney Collection   111

*The illustrations on pages 11, 37, 47, 65, 73, 93 are by
William K. Plummer*

SBN: 698-30525-6
SBN: 698-20273-2
Library of Congress Catalog Card Number: 74-76235
PRINTED IN THE UNITED STATES OF AMERICA

Contents

Introduction

This book is fictionalized biography. There are dialogues and scenes unauthenticated but as common to the frontier as the beginning and ending of its ever-changing days. Much of the fabric of this story has been picked, a line here, another there, from the fifteen volumes of Abraham Lincoln's own writing. Much, too, has been gathered from the author's own Lincoln collection comprising 472 volumes.

The language of the frontier was earthy and expressive. Some of the words have rightly lost favor, Injun, for example. But in Abe Lincoln's time it was a part of everyday speech used even by those who sympathized with the Indians' plight. Today this is seen as a derogatory term, but to create the real atmosphere of Abe's world, colloquialisms and the spoken language of the time and place seems a necessary ingredient.

"Mastery of language may have been that ultimate factor without which he would have failed," writes Benjamin P. Thomas of Lincoln. "Esteem for the rhythmic beauty that may be coaxed from language . . . endowed him with the faculty to write well and speak well. . . ."

But throughout his life Lincoln held onto much of the earthy speech of the frontier. News reporters, not understanding, made repeated reference to his "crude manner of speech." Most of the material in quotation marks in the present writing has been culled from the many letters he wrote to people such as Leonard Sweet and Joshua Speed, who, like him, understood the language of the frontier hearth and crossroads store. In addition to Lincoln's own writings, the journals of frontier visitors such as Sarah Hopkins, Morris Birkbeck, William Cullen Bryant, and others afford a wealth of material from which the popular expression of the day was gathered.

This is indeed a very simple story: the developing years of a boy named Abraham Lincoln set in the real atmosphere and environment of his day rather than the legendary world which it later became. It is one teacher's attempt to re-create the climate in which the seeds were sown in the heart of a boy, seeds which sprouted, grew, and flowered in the heart of the man, Abraham Lincoln.

CHAPTER ONE

"They'll Laff at My Breeches"

On a May morning in 1815, Sarah, almost nine, urged her reluctant brother, Abe, aged six and a half, along the road from their cabin toward the log school a mile and a half northward on the Louisville and Nashville Turnpike. The turnpike was no more than a trail, wide enough for a wagon.

"It's worth it," Tom Lincoln had said as he and his wife, Nancy, sat before the fire of their Knob Creek farm talking to Reuben Helm, who had five children and had started the movement to "git uh school."

"Pears to me it's a precious barg'in," Nancy added. "I've always had soul hunger for larning, but I ain't never had the chance I want my young'uns to git."

"With a newspaper comin' from Lexington and Louisville every week, the time's gonna come when a man's gotta be eddicated," added Reuben Helm. "If a man can handle readin' law and the Scripters, and figer in writin', it ain't likely he'll be took easy, I always say."

So Tom and Nancy Lincoln had subscribed a penny a day for each child, plus no more than three additional charges of five cents each for supplies. The length of the term would be eighty days. The subscribers would "board around" (house and feed) the teacher. If this caused a hardship to some, they could make "a poundin' " (a reasonable contribution of meat and flour) instead of "takin' in the teacher."

Teachers of the subscription schools were mainly wanderers who came for a season or two and moved on. Being boarded and housed around from house to house for a week or two must have been a shallow, baseless existence indeed, appealing only to the totally dedicated or the shiftless charlatan in search of lodging. The latter was soon exposed, while the former might find himself a virtual slave, stuck with a family of five or six children and a father who felt that "extry larnin'," after chores were done, should delight both teacher and pupils, not to mention the father's ambition to "larn readin' " so he could go into "pollerticks." And indeed it was a rare house where the teacher did not sleep in a room with the children and frequently in the same bed with one or two of them. The best bet for a good teacher was the home-based teacher—that is, one who lived permanently where he taught.

Abe and Sarah spotted the log school which had been built by the men of the dozen or more families who lived between Knob Creek and Athersonville. The building was located, according to one of Lincoln's schoolmates, "on a little elevation about a hundred yards up a little run or holler on the left as you go toward Athersonville."

Thomas Lincoln and his neighbors probably built the schoolhouse in two or three days. The logs could be cut in one. And since they were not hewn smooth on any side, the building could be "raised" complete with roof and mud-and-stick lath chimney and fireplace in another day or two.

There was only a dirt floor in the twelve-foot-square structure. One of the neighbors contributed a bearskin to cover the door opening. Two small windows for light were left without oilskin or shutters. Inside the school, butternut logs had been split in half and put on puncheons (large peglike legs) to serve as benches and writing desks.

Sarah found her little brother as slow as one of her father's reluctant yoke oxen. Abe was not anxious to go among strange people. But worse than that, he was wearing his first pair of linsey-woolsey pants and felt awkward and embarrassed.

Boys on the frontier wore "shirttails," a single long garment, also called tow shirts. But at the age of six or seven a boy graduated to pants. Some boys also acquired their first

11

wool hat at this time, but a coonskin cap was even more prized. Abe felt right from the neck up, wearing his soft coonskin cap over his coarse black hair, but the new home-made shirt and pants reaching down to his bare feet were strange.

Sarah and Abe didn't carry books, slates, or fancy lunch boxes. The only book in the Lincoln cabin was the "old dog-eared arithmetic," but Mr. Riney, the teacher, hadn't sent word to bring books and "tracts."

Very few pioneer children owned books or slates. The teacher supplied the scanty assortment of books—sometimes not three copies of the same book could be found in the whole school. Often the only new reading materials for the older children were religious tracts distributed by wandering preachers.

For lunch, Abe carried a piece of salt pork folded into a slab of corn dodger. It was wrapped in oil paper. This oil paper would be re-used many times. Sarah carried a similar lunch, as did most of the dozen or more children who attended the school.

As Sarah and Abe came closer to the log building, several dogs ran to meet them. A pig or two also grunted a greeting. Dogs and pigs followed frontier children wherever they went, causing no little annoyance to both schoolmasters and "camp meetin' " preachers. The sound of mingled voices came out to the Lincoln children. Although they were early, some people were already studying aloud. In the frontier school there was usually no bell to call school's beginning. As the pupils arrived, each would begin some task of learning assigned by the teacher.

"They'll laff at my breeches," Abe kept whispering to Sarah, who was two years older than Abe and felt so respon-

12

sible that she was holding onto his buckskin shirt to keep him from backing off and running away.

"Ain't nobody gonna laff," she whispered in exasperation. "Come on, Abe, or I'll drag you like a scairt pig." And with that she pushed the bearskin aside so as to not make any noise and pulled Abe through the doorway, letting go of his shirt as soon as they were inside so she wouldn't create a commotion.

Before Abe had a chance to look around the walls and up and down the rows of puncheoned benches, he was looking up into the beckoning eyes of a "giant of a man," much taller than Abe's five-foot-ten-inch father. The man folded one of his big hands around Sarah's, saying, "I'm Zachariah Riney. I'm your teacher." He held his other hand out, and Abe put out his right hand the way his Ma had taught him to do when Preacher Jesse Head, who had married Abe's parents, came to make a "pastoral call." Abe's Pa had told him to "give a man a firm grip, so he can feel it in his heart."

Zachariah Riney was born in Maryland and there received his grammar schooling. After emigrating to Bardstown, Kentucky, he studied under Father Stephen Theodore Badin. Father Badin had come from Europe with the education of the best French universities for a background and landed at Baltimore, Maryland, during the Revolution. He was ordained there in 1791—the first priest ordained within the thirteen original states. At the time he was twenty-five years of age and spoke only a few words of English. Immediately after his ordination he was sent to the "dark and bloody ground" of Kentucky to plant and cultivate the seeds of faith. He settled in Bardstown, 16 miles north of Knob Creek.

Joined soon after his arrival by the rough and saintly

13

Father Nerincks, who had also been educated in Europe, the two became legend. Austere and indefatigable, living largely in the saddle as they covered their far-flung and dangerous circuits, they cut and rolled logs to build chapels and schools, whipped bullies who tried to drive them out of the land, and taught the Indians to use midwives at childbirth instead of sending their women into the woods alone to have their children.

At Bardstown, Fathers Badin and Nerincks founded schools. Mr. Riney had studied at the school in Bardstown. Abe, Sarah, the Helms, Haycrofts, and other children would spend eighty days of their lives with him.

The term Abe and his sister were beginning this May morning in 1815 started after the corn and pumpkins had been planted. The summer term began after "plantin' time" and lasted for about eight weeks till berry-pickin' time. Although the age range in the twelve-by-twelve log school would be from about six to twenty-one, the summer term would be made up mainly of the younger children. The older ones would hoe and weed during the summer and attend the winter or fall term, which began after "corn gathering" and lasted about two months, until winter brought cold winds whistling through the unchinked logs of the schoolhouse. Few children had clothing or moccasins sufficiently warm to brave the wind and snow walking to school. As the autumn winds grew colder and colder, the crude benches were moved closer and closer to the fireplace. Some frontier schools lacked even this luxury.

The frontier schools, typical of the one Abe and his sister attended, were called ABC, or blab, schools: ABC because of the rudimentary nature of what was offered, and blab because all the pupils studied aloud, arithmetic, spelling, reading all being done aloud by different people at the same time. Anyone not working aloud was assumed to be loafing. The keen eye of the teacher would spot the silent and apply the rod—lightly across the shoulders of the girls, but without reservation to the boys.

The blab schools probably constituted one of the world's most effective mills for developing the power to concentrate. It demonstrated actively for the child the music that can be coaxed from language. This, which became such a significant and lasting product of Lincoln's education, began in the blab school.

Throughout Abe's entire life he read aloud to himself. In later years, when he wrote his poetic and deathless utterances, he sounded each word aloud as he wrote.

Learning began with the ABC's and was limited to an elementary knowledge of reading, writing, and ciphering (ciphering being arithmetic). The older children spent much of their own time helping the younger with their lessons, all drilling and studying aloud.

The value of this communal effort probably had no little part in making the frontier a place where men, though often living great distances apart, did not feel alone. In this cooperative effort the older children provided themselves with two of the best learning processes: learning by doing and learning by teaching. Not infrequently an eighteen- or nineteen-year-old boy or girl, having gone through all the books available two or three times, would attend the "after corn gathering" session to assist the schoolmaster. This gave them a chance to read any new books the schoolmaster may have acquired. Many who returned at this age wanted to become teachers themselves.

Abe would find that he was no different from the other

boys who had been born to the demanding, sometimes exciting and pleasant, sometimes foreboding and cruel life of the frontier.

Years later, when Lincoln had made more of his frontier opportunities for education than not even the fondest parent or a guardian angel would have dreamed of for him on this May morning, men would search his background for some inborn quality or legacy that gave his learning depth and power above that of his contemporaries and made him their leader. They found no magic quality.

What they found was sturdy stock, pioneer fortitude, respectability, and above-average accomplishment, coming down through seven Lincoln generations from the first to land on the shores of the American wilderness in 1637. For in that year Samuel Lincoln, a weaver's apprentice, aged seventeen, arrived with his master, one Francis Lawes, at Old Salem, in the Massachusetts colony.

Within two years Samuel moved to Hingham, where his brothers, Thomas and Daniel, had since arrived and settled. There Samuel Lincoln married and became the father of eleven children. One of these eleven, Abe's great-grandfather, Mordecai, moved in the vanguard of pioneer Americans, who were establishing themselves in Pennsylvania, New Jersey, then Virginia, and finally Kentucky.

One of the first stories of his family that Abe remembered—and it was repeated often to visitors as they sat before the Lincoln fireplace—was the story of his grandfather Abraham.

Daniel Boone's stories of the land beyond the mountains —black soil and green grass, tall timber and streams

16

aplenty—began to stir a yearning in the heart of Grandfather Abraham.

Linville, in Rockingham County, Virginia, was becoming too crowded. Houses were already being built in sight of each other, and people began to say "the time's acomin' when a man won't be able to call his own hogs without fetchin' his neighbor's." One of these people was Abraham Lincoln's grandfather. So in 1780 he made a trip into Kentucky to "spy out the land."

Two years later, having purchased several thousands of acres in Jefferson County, east of Louisville, the senior Abraham Lincoln and his wife, Bathsheba, sold their land in Rockingham County, Virginia, and took the Wilderness Road down the Shenandoah Valley to Cumberland Gap and thence into Kentucky.

On a May morning four years later, 1786, Abraham Lincoln was shot by an Indian. The six-year-old boy who was at his father's side when he fell was Thomas Lincoln, the youngest son, saved by the quick thinking and sure aim of an older brother, Mordecai, who shot the Indian as he came from the woods to carry off the child. From his father Abe had heard the story often—half in wonder, half in sorrow.

CHAPTER TWO

"*But Apple Butter Is Better*"

Mr. Riney introduced Abe to the world of ABC's and numbers. He widened Abe's narrow wilderness horizon with his readings and stories. One of the older Helm or Perceful girls heard a new column of multiplication or spelling in a corner of the room whenever the teacher was ready. Abe wasn't always ready with his spelling column and would have to spell some words over ten times aloud and then write them five times on a slate. When he had learned one column perfectly, he went on to the next.

Each scholar moved at his own pace, and except for some of the older boys who didn't come to school often and usually dropped out altogether, competition was keen. "It's not how much talent you've got," Mr. Riney would say, "it's what you do with it." Then he would tell a story:

"A certain rich man, going on a long journey, called his servants together and gave them each a talent. Now a talent was a large sum of money. 'When I come back,' he said, 'I will see what each of you has done with his talent.' When he returned, he found one servant who had done nothing, others who had used theirs to varying degrees of success, and one who had doubled his. He was so angry at the servant who had done nothing that he took his talent away and gave it to the one who had made the most of his. Some of the people thought this was pretty mean. So the man who had given out the talents explained it this way: 'If you work hard, you will get even more than you expect to get, and if you don't work hard, you won't even be able to keep that which you have.' " And then Mr. Riney would repeat, "It's not how much talent you've got, it's what you do with it."

One of Mr. Riney's stories was about his former teacher, Father Nerincks. Father Nerincks began a long search for Betty Miles, who had been carried north by the Indians. Following one lead after another and riding the wilderness for months at a time, he found her after six years in the great north woods (later to become the state of Michigan), paid her ransom to the Indians, and took her home.

Then Mr. Riney would turn to a story in the Bible and begin to read: "What man having a hundred sheep, and one of them goes astray, does not leave the ninety and nine and go into the mountains, and seek the one that has gone astray."

Even the youngest frontier child knew how "aggravatin'" and worrisum" it could be when a "skiddish" heifer went over the stump-and-brush fence and disappeared in the wilds or when one of the shoats being "fattened for butcher" didn't come from mast feedin', fattening on acorns in the forest. An animal not found before nightfall was a "goner for good."

This was one of Abe's favorite stories. After telling such a story, Zachariah Riney would relate it to the Bible and help his students remember Biblical teachings by relating them to their own experiences.

After twenty-five days of schooling, Sarah and some of the children had finished their "first" columns, had read the three little books over twice, and moved up to one big book with real stories and another big book with grammar to learn and sentences to write.

One book found in all schools of the day was Dilworth's Speller. Whether Abe's father bought a copy is doubtful, but it was the one book, next to the Bible, that most often found its way into frontier homes. Mr. Riney might have used some of the "supplies" money to provide enough copies so that the scholars from each family could use it at home at least twice a week.

Often Mr. Riney's students would fight "tooth and claw" to stand up the longest in a "spelling bee," hoping to win the right to pick any book in the school "to keep over Sunday."

Dilworth's Speller, though perhaps already used by the pitch-pine light two nights during the week, was the prize most often chosen by the child whose cabin did not possess one. Many a thoughtful pioneer parent, having listened to a child working aloud from the book, would say: "Thar's a whole eddication in that book."

A New Guide to the English Tongue was the real title of the book, written in 1740 by Thomas Dilworth, an English schoolmaster. It was popular in England for more than sixty years. In the American colonies it was the leading elementary textbook, and it continued to be popular until long after the Revolution, when Noah Webster's Old Blue-backed Speller replaced it.

It was a complete study of the art of communication, both written and oral. It was a combination speller, reader,

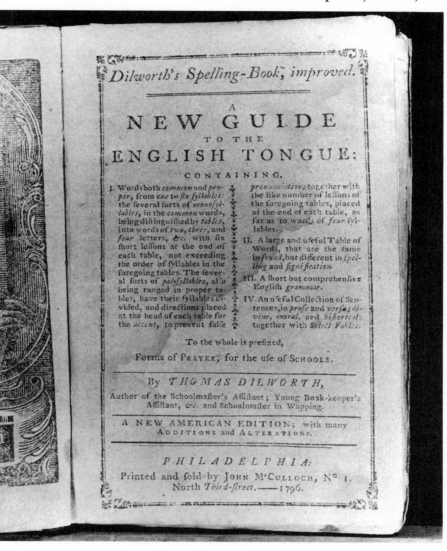

Dilworth's Spelling-Book, improved.

A

NEW GUIDE

TO THE

ENGLISH TONGUE:

CONTAINING,

I. Words both *common* and *proper*, from *one* to *fix fyllables*: the several forts of *monofyllables*, in the *common* words, being diftinguifhed by *tables*, into words of *two, three*, and *four* letters, &c. with fix fhort leffons at the end of each table, not exceeding the order of fyllables in the foregoing tables. The several forts of *polyfyllables*, alfo being ranged in proper tables, have their fyllables divided, and directions placed at the head of each table for the *accent*, to prevent falfe *pronunciation*; together with the like number of leffons of the foregoing tables, placed at the end of each table, as far as to words of *four* fyllables.

II. A large and ufeful Table of Words, that are the fame in *found*, but different in *fpelling* and *fignification*.

III. A fhort but comprehenfive English *grammar*.

IV. An ufeful Collection of Sentences, in *profe* and *verfe; divine, moral*, and *hiftorical*; together with *Select Fables*.

To the whole is prefixed,

Forms of PRAYER, for the ufe of SCHOOLS.

By *THOMAS DILWORTH*,

Author of the Schoolmafter's Affiftant; Young Book-keeper's Affiftant, &c. and Schoolmafter in Wapping.

A NEW AMERICAN EDITION; with many ADDITIONS and ALTERATIONS.

PHILADELPHIA:

Printed and fold by JOHN M'CULLOCH, N° 1. North *Third-ftreet.*——1796.

grammar, manual of morals, and devotional. Morals made up the writing exercises, and prayers were arranged for various occasions, such as birth and death, illness and poverty, planting time and harvest, as well as prayers for wayward boys and misers. It contained lists of synonyms, homonyms, and antonyms with sentence exercises for each. There were fables and stories designed to teach proper conduct and ways of dealing justly with one's fellowman. Writing exercises included useful definitions, axioms, and historical facts. Except for mathematics—and indeed it included instruction in how to count to 100 in Roman numerals—the child who mastered old Dilworth, dog-eared, worn and re-covered with oilcloth or gingham though it might be, learned more of writing and speaking than is often taught in the first ten years of public education today.

M O R A L   T A L E S.

The CHILD *and the* SERPENT.

From Fiske's *The New England Spelling-book.*

So when it was Abe's turn to have a copy of Dilworth's Speller for the night, he copied out such things as:

Q. What is Grammar?
A. Grammar is the science of letters, or the art of writing and speaking syntactically.

Dot the i.

rat, rate; rid, ride; rob, robe; rot, rote; van, vane.
I wage no war.
Bid him bide with us and dine.
A manly youth.
Never mimic thy master.
Do not be tardy.
Amend your way of life.
Be polite.
Delay not.
I love the humane.
Uplift the lowly.
Starboard is the right-hand side of a ship; larboard, the left.
On me when dunces are satiric, I take it for a panegyric.
Brevity is the soul of wit.
This transitory life.
Do right, come what may.
He suffered torments.
Peaceable neighbors.
Fulfill your promise.
Your welfare shall be my concern.
What's everybody's business is nobody's business.
Mind your books.

Q. What is humility?

A. A lowly temper of mind.

Q. What are the advantages of humility?

A. The advantages of humility in this life are very numerous and great. The humble man has few or no enemies. Everyone loves him and is ready to do him good.

The second most important textbook in Mr. Riney's school was Pike's "Arithmetick." It was written by Nicolas Pike, a native of New Hampshire and a graduate of Harvard College. Pike was a civil engineer and also a "home-based teacher." His arithmetic, published in 1788, was the first mathematics book written in America. Its 300 pages of small print provided thousands of young Americans with all they ever knew of "cipherin'." Indeed, it contained about all there *was* to know about "cipherin'," both theoretically and practically. Word problems were designed to teach honesty, justice, and fair play, as well as decimal, interest, and root. A whole essay on the value and preciousness of time could be extracted from problems beginning with: If a man worked . . .? How much time is lost if . . .? What would be the value of his time in dollars and cents if . . . ? It contained chapters on wet and dry weights and measures, dealt with barter and even touched on the mathematics of probability. Being written by a civil engineer, it used surveying in its approach to many problems. It began with elementary work and moved forward lesson by lesson. Each student went at his own pace.

Whatever excitement there was in "cipherin'," from Pike's "Arithmetick," a difficulty of equal dimension pre-

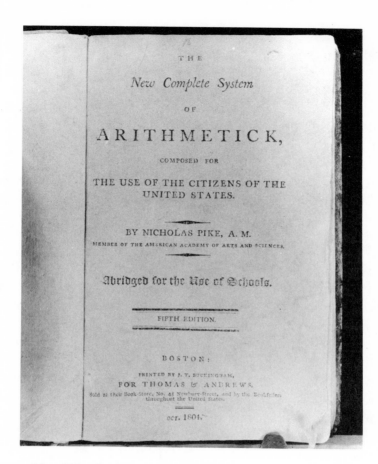

sented itself in finding something to write on, and with, both at home and at school. Paper was almost nonexistent, but if a letter came from some relative in the East, any space that wasn't written on would be used until there was no room left for a single word or number. Slate, or a smooth piece of whipsawed pine board and a piece of charcoal were the most commonly used writing materials. When Abe had written, "Things are dear," he would scrape the

25

pine clean with a jackknife and write, "Behold the sun" or "Hallow the day." Crude slates were made from pieces of shale, and soapstone could be easily whittled into pencil shape. Soapstone ranged in color from blue-black to light yellow, and a lucky student might have three or four different colored slate pencils. Slates could be ordered from Lexington or Louisville, but most people made their own, as they did almost everything they used. Pens were made from the tail or wing feathers of buzzards or wild turkeys. Ink was made by boiling blackberry briar root in a copper pan. Light-colored soapstone on the back of a fire shovel was also good for "practice writin'."

"We have to get a lot from a little," was Zachariah Riney's classroom axiom, repeated almost daily as he tried to make books and slates go around. "There's more to be found at every reading," he would say in reply to the disappointed look from a boy or girl starting Aesop's *Fables* or *The Kentucky Preceptor* for the third time.

Besides books and slates, the only other learning aids were Mr. Riney's birch rod and a large slate in a wooden frame, hung against one wall of the room. Mr. Riney used his birch rod mainly for pointing to words, or "ciphers," on the slate, but sometimes it whacked on the shoulders of a buckskin shirt and brought one of the big boys back to his "recitin'."

Abe paid close attention to what was put on Mr. Riney's slate. It wasn't much wider and higher than a cabin window, and sometimes a careless writer would start a big word like "Transylvania" or "constitution" at one side and run clear off the edge on the other without finishing the word. Mr. Riney could get whole short sentences on one line and

26

enough sentences from top to bottom to make a whole "lesson."

Some of the lessons were Mr. Riney's thoughts on neighborliness, cruelty, worship, patience, government, nature, solitude, pride, and happiness. Mr. Riney would tell what the Bible says about neighborliness. He might also recite a poem on the subject or tell a story about how someone saved his neighbor's life or cow. Then when all of the older boys and girls had said what they thought about neighborliness, Mr. Riney would pick one scholar to go up to the slateboard and write "the heart of the matter."

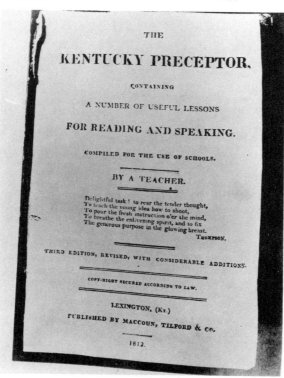

Abe's eyes would stray from his "columns," for now the fun began—for everybody except the poor scholar at the slateboard. One long, wobbly sentence would fill up half the slate. Then Mr. Riney would say, "A short man can tote a long roof pole if he's strong enough. We can't cut the roof pole off, but we can shorten up the man and put some muscle on him so he won't wobble so much. This is what we call making a short phrase carry a long thought."

Then he would rub out all except three or four words of the sentence. "Now," he would say, "let's hitch two more long thoughts to this one and we'll have a three-horse wagon. And everybody knows a three-horse wagon can carry more than a one-horse or a two-horse wagon."

When Mr. Riney had helped the scholar make the "short words carry long thoughts," Abe thought some of Mr. Riney's sentences were like the ones in the speller: "Young and old, rich and poor, wise and ignorant, will appear before the judgment seat."

At home Abe would pester Sarah to help him put long thoughts into short words. On the smooth pine board in charcoal he would copy phrases from the speller: "Things are dear, behold the sun, hallow the day." "Fulfill your promise, do not be tardy, mind your books." "Unite with the good, shun the unjust, amend your way of life."

"Back home in Maryland my grandparents made apple butter," Mr. Riney would say. "My Pa has told me about it often. One day Johnny Appleseed's trees will start bearing and you'll be making apple butter. Early in the morning, on apple-butter-making day, a big copper kettle, big enough to hold two or three bushels of quartered apples was hung on the kettle iron outside, over a roaring fire. Then all day

28

long more apples were added, maybe five or six bushels in all. All the time the kettle was stirred with a wooden stirrer on a long handle so the one stirring wouldn't have to stand too close to the fire. Everybody took a turn so the bottom wouldn't stick. About midday a light yellowish pink color would begin to show on top of the kettle. 'Applesauce,' my grandmother would say, 'I'll skim off a mess or two. Not much, it doesn't have much body, too much water.'

"Long after the last cut apples had been added, the pink would begin to turn to red and get darker and darker as the boiling down continued. Sometimes the boiling down had to be done until sunset or later. When the bubbles broke rich-red on the surface, my grandfather would say, 'Let the fire die down now.' Then when the fire had died down and bubbles stopped the blob-blob that had been sounding at the top of the kettle all day, my grandfather, trusting no one else, would give the final stirring to get the hidden bubbles. 'One bubble can spoil a whole gallon crock,' he would say. 'Starts green mold from the inside.'

"They didn't care much for the applesauce. That's why my grandmother dipped out only a mess or two. But they mightily favored the rich, heavy red apple butter, boiled down to gallons from bushels.

"Brought up from the cellar where it was stored in crocks and jars against the winter, they spread it on their bread at breakfast, dinner, and supper and never tired of it. 'What's for tapering off?' my grandfather would say, meaning what's for dessert? And my grandmother would say, 'Apple butter.'

"Applesauce is good, but apple butter is better. So we want to learn to boil down a bushel basket of words until they fit into a gallon crock with the lid on tight. Just like

29

offals and fat don't amount to much at butchering time, but they're mighty useful rendered down to smooth white lard. It's like separating 'the wheat from the chaff,' as the Bible says. The slateboard isn't much for long thoughts, but it's mighty useful for long thoughts boiled down."

Only the older boys and girls who had finished Dilworth's Speller and were reading *The Kentucky Preceptor* were sent to the front of the room to write on the slateboard. "They're mighty lucky," young Abe said to Sarah as they walked home toward Knob Creek, "to git to write on the slateboard every day."

Abe had just lodged a well-aimed rock into the bottom of a squirrel's nest and sent three young squirrels scampering to the tallest branches of a "pople tree," squealing danger as they went.

"Luckier than them young 'uns," Sarah answered in disgust. "If the crows and blue jays start screamin' danger, their mother won't come back, and a owl will git 'em."

"It's a mighty big favor" was Abe's way of saying that writing on the slateboard was a great privilege. "Ev'n if I ain't finished the speller, I could try. I sure like hitchin' words together."

"It ain't much of a favor when Mr. Riney rubs off what's been writ and the writer gits flustered," Sarah replied.

"No matter," Abe said. "I'm gonna stay on the lookout of short words for long thoughts and bile 'em down the way Mr. Riney says." Years later at Gettsyburg, Abraham Lincoln would use Mr. Riney's lesson and put thoughts that will last as long as time into 287 short words.

CHAPTER THREE

"*Abe's Head Is Festerin' with Questions*"

Tom and Nancy Lincoln had asked Mr. Riney "to cum fur a meal" when the school session was over. This was their way of saying that they were "powerful pleased." They had paid up their subscription and three five-cent payments for supplies.

Mr. Riney must have been pleased too for he gave Sarah and Abe a copy of Dilworth's Speller, "too worn for more scholar use," he said, "but with a little stitchin' it'll hold together for home use." When Mr. Riney was ready to leave after the meal, Nancy Lincoln made Abe wash his hands in the pan that sat on the bench outside the cabin door so he could shake hands and thank Mr. Riney. Sarah's hands were clean, but washing didn't change Abe's much. "The walnut husk stain will wear off," he told his mother. Mr. Riney wrapped his big warm hand around Abe's to say good-bye. Abe was wonderin' if Mr. Riney would ever give away his big slateboard, but if he did, he'd give it to one of the bigger boys or girls.

"It's mighty wore," Tom Lincoln said after Mr. Riney

had left, folding the ragged speller in his leathery hands. "But thar's a heap of larnin' thar yet. Stitch it up with some moccasin string."

Later, when chores were done and everybody had "et," Nancy Lincoln took the big needle and thread, used mainly for sewing moccasins, and stitched together the backless pages of the book which Abe hadn't quite "larned" enough of to get to write on Mr. Riney's slateboard.

Abe sat in the doorway, looking at the corn shocks. They looked like wigwams, and when the harvest moon passed a cloud and darkened the field, Abe thought there might be Indians behind them. The warm October breeze blew the smell of harvest in through the cabin doorway and tapped the open door lightly against the side of the cabin, swaying on its strap hinges. He listened carefully to the last few verses of his mother's song as she stitched by the pine-knot light:

Oh, what is heavier than the lead?
And the devil said I gather the dead.
And what is better than the bread?
And the crow called "caw" from the Judas tree.

Oh, grief is heavier than the lead.
And the devil said I burn the dead.
God's blessing's better than the bread,
And the crow fell out of the Judas tree.

Now you have answered one less nine.
You still are God's, you're none of mine.
I'll take the crow for its stealing crime.
There's one more question, but not this time.

32

"It's a pretty song, but mighty fearful," said Abe's father.

Abe didn't want to sit in the doorway any longer. There was a rustlin' in the corn shocks. He pulled the door shut after him and it swung lopsided into place, leaving a crack at the top through which Abe could see the moon and stars almost close enough to touch the treetops at the edge of the clearing.

"What's a Judas tree?" he asked when he was safe inside. "I ain't never heard of such a tree 'round here."

"It's the same as a redbud," said Abe's father, "Ma, tell 'em why it's called the Judas tree. You know it better'n I do."

"They say," Nancy Lincoln began, "that the cross of Jesus was made out of redbud tree wood. And when Jesus was hung on it and died, it had betrayed Him like Judas, so people began to call it the Judas tree. Before it was used to make the cross, it wasn't a bloomin' tree, but after's the drop of Jesus' blood had been spilt on it, they were never the same. The redbud trees began to bloom every year, but the blooms never opened. They just stayed ever after, in little round buds like drops of blood."

"I know 'em," Abe broke in. "There's some in the dogwoods at the edge of the cow lot."

"There's a tale about dogwoods, too. What is it, Tom?" Abe's mother asked.

"I forgit. I was ponderin' what Preacher Jesse Head said the devil's ninth question is. He 'lows how the devil knows the question, but even the devil don't know the answer. Preacher Head 'lows the question is, 'What is the time a clock can't tell?' And Preacher Head says that time is 'when

33

TOM LINCOLN

a person's time has come, when the Lord calls, and even the devil don't know that. The devil himself is smarter'n anybody but God. So the devil ain't gonna ask no question he ain't got no slick answer to.' "

34

The moon had climbed above the crack over the cabin door. But a couple of stars were still there, "close and watchful and comfortin'," thought Abe. From out beyond the corn patch the "hoo-hoo" of a hoot owl interrupted Abe's listening and caused shivers to run up and down his spine.

When owls raided the roostin' trees of a settler's chickens and the lonesome hoots came on the night winds, they had meaning for young Abe. "If an owl steals a chicken in daylight, it's gonna be a hard winter. If an owl hoots in a dooryard tree, somebody'n that house'll die before the next full moon."

With his Pa talking about "the devil, and a person's time comin, and all them puzzlin' things" Abe was fearful, but "it's fur enough away not to worry," he thought to himself, and went back to listening to his father.

"What puzzles the devil, Preacher Jesse Head says, is God's elect. That's what predestination means. That God has picked out who is His elect before their time has come, and the devil ain't got no way of knowin'. And here's how it works, says Preacher Jesse. A man can be dead drunk, gallopin' his horse and the devil watchin'. The horse stumbles and the devil says, 'I got 'im,' 'cause he sees the man is gonna break his neck against the butt of a big white oak tree. What the devil don't know is that on the way down there's a sober second when the man repents and he's God's, 'cause he's God's elect. So the devil loses. That's what preacher Head says about what the devil's question is that he won't never ask. And that's where that song, 'Between the saddle and the ground,/He pardon sought and pardon found' comes from. If that's the way it goes."

35

"The world is powerful mysterious," said Nancy Lincoln. "You children must handle this book careful. I've done the best I can. Now git to bed. Say your prayers, too."

"I need a drink of water, but I'm fear'd to go out," said Abe.

Tom Lincoln got up, and Abe followed him through the cabin door. Outside, his father took a gourd dipper from where it hung above the bench, dipped it in a wooden bucket, and gave it to Abe.

Tom Lincoln took in the sky and the horizon with a studied look. "Dry air. It'll be a good shuckin' day."

Abe looked at the still wigwamlike shocks of corn and thought he saw things moving. He looked at the dark rim of forest that encircled his narrow and simple world and saw things—vast, endless, mysterious, lit by moon and stars, confusing, and "powerful puzzlin'."

He slipped past his Pa and went back into the cabin. Nestled down in his shuck tick, he said his prayers in a half whisper, so Sarah could hear and wouldn't call, "Ma, Abe ain't sayin' his prayers":

> Now I lay me down to sleep.
> I pray the Lord my soul to keep.
> If I should die before I wake,
> I pray the Lord my soul to take.

"Why just ask God to save you if you die before you wake?" he whispered to Sarah.

" 'Cause you wouldn't be wake to ask Him. If'en you die in the day, you kin ask right then."

Abe's thoughts drifted to the spring on the Nolin Creek

36

farm where they lived before moving to the new farm on Knob Creek. Here Abe toddled behind his mother to the spring. Later he carried his side of the bucket with Sarah. The spring came out of a cave in the hillside, and natives called it the Mine Spring. The moss-covered limestone arch was high enough for a man to walk under, but Abe was never tempted to wade in. What lurked far back in the darkness was uncertain, mysterious, and "fearsum." The sparkling stream just kept "comin' and comin'." From where? They called that farm the Sinkin' Spring Farm because the spring sank back into a limestone crevice and disappeared into the earth only a few feet from the mouth of the cave.

Then he remembered his brother, Thomas, who died in infancy a few months before the family moved from Sinking Spring to Knob Creek.

Before Abe's father whipsawed a log into boards and pegged together the pine coffin in which he buried little Thomas at the Little Mount Primitive Baptist Church, he sawed two thin butt ends from the round log. After little Thomas was buried, he took the round butts and the pieces of board which were left and made Abe a cart "strong enough to haul fire sticks and water." Tom Lincoln didn't know how to tell Abe that "life must go on," and Abe wouldn't have understood anyway. But Tom Lincoln could show him.

After his brother died, Abe wanted to ask questions about heaven, but his mother looked sad and puzzled as she went about her work. So he listened to her song and kept quiet:

> Jesus is a rock in a weary land,
> A weary land, a weary land;
> Jesus is a rock in a weary land,
> A shelter in the time of storm.

Abe listened too when his parents puzzled over the death of their "young'un," as they sat before the fire after Abe and Sarah had gone to bed. Abe wasn't afraid, for "there ain't no ghosts of children," he had heard. But when an older person died, it was "scary," for their ghosts came back as "haunts and pestered the livin'."

His mother often sat by the fire perplexed and still, and there were long quiet spells when she was "jus' thinkin'."

38

"What will be will be" was God's reason. But she looked for some earthly reason, too. Had she violated one of the numberless superstitions that spelled life or death, good or evil, sickness or health for her child? She had stayed away from Thomas Lincoln's horses for if a horse breathed on a pregnant woman, evil would come to the child. During her pregnancy Thomas had milked the cow for if a pregnant woman was kicked by a cow, the child would be deformed—sometimes stillborn with the head of a calf. She had sent little Sarah ahead of her on the path to the spring, for if a pregnant woman saw a snake, the child would stammer. Careful that no bird flew into the cabin, that no wood from a tree struck by lightning was burned on the fire while she was pregnant, (for these would bring death to the child), she had tried also not to think too much of the infant or ask the sex or color of the child's hair before the midwife, Aunt Peggy Walters, had washed it, for this too would cause it to die.

Signs, dreams, and puzzlin' sayings flowed in the environmental mainstream of Abe Lincoln's education. There were, of course, the Ten Commandments, but there were other commandments. The precariousness of the human condition, expressed in the basic primitive poetry of superstitions, was a part of his upbringing. Some of these he carried with him throughout his life.

Side by side in the dark recesses of his mind Abe stored "Thou shalt not kill" and "If you carry a shovel into the cabin, it'll be used next to dig a grave." He knew "Honor thy father and mother" and "If a dog howls in front of a cabin door three nights in a row, in the dark of the moon, a coffin will be carried out before the next full moon." He learned that a camp meetin' and a cabin raisin' were "pretty much alike." The Bible said, "You must earn your living by the sweat of your brow," and his Pa said, "Ain't nobody gonna give you nothin'. If you gonna be anything, you gonna make it yourself."

The new mysteries which he encountered stretched from the mystery-filled arc of the horizon in upon him to the narrow circle of the fireside. Young Abe Lincoln, and the unnumbered frontier children like him, learned at a very early age that there were signs in these mysteries—good signs and bad signs. They developed acute powers of seeing and listening. Danger was never farther away than the edge of the path to the spring, the other side of the chicken pen, or the border of the corn lot. The mournful and plaintive wail of the screech owl, the ominous "Who's next?" question in the "hoo-hoo" of the hoot owl, and the omen of the timber wolf's howl "with a heifer loose in the woods" accented and punctuated the dark grandeur of silence where a child learned to listen and listened to learn.

In this world of superstitions, signs, dark forebodings, hope for a brighter day, a better season next year, or a farm where the clearin' would be easier and the ground more fertile, Abe grew, did his chores, and filled his idle hours with wonder. He learned to weigh the "good signs" against the "bad signs" with faith in the belief that "if the sun goeth down it also riseth." "And these surroundings," wrote William H. Herndon, who knew that world and was a product of it, "helped to create that unique character which in the eyes of a great portion of the American people was only less curious and amusing than it was august and noble."

All the talk around the Lincoln fireside was not of a solemn nature. Thomas Lincoln was said to be a thoughtful man. He must also have been "good company," for he drew not only his neighbors—the Enlows, Brownlees, Gallahers, and Cessanas—but men such as Preacher Jesse Head and Christopher Columbus Graham, who had attended Tom Lincoln's wedding and was one of the most colorful characters on the Kentucky frontier. Preacher Head had married Tom and Nancy Lincoln and remained a close friend. His preachin' circuit carried him into the wilderness of Tennessee, Ohio, and Indiana, from which came new stories to be told around the Lincoln fireside. On the banks of the Ohio River he had met Johnny Appleseed, dressed in his coffee sack, talking with angels, refusing to kill a hornet that stung him because it was one of "God's critters." "So peculiar a man ain't 'peared on earth since John the

Baptist," said Preacher Head. When Preacher Head showed up in the clearing, riding his rawboned roan mare, his saddlebags stuffed with religious tracts and a new bottle of "just liniment" for Tom Lincoln to ease muscles strained from stump pullin', little Abe hurried through his chores so he wouldn't miss "none of Preacher Head's talk." Among the stories which Jesse Head told and retold was how he converted the aged Cherokee chieftain Dragging Canoe to Christianity and then lost him when Jesse Head's God failed to drive away thousands of passenger pigeons that swooped down on the Cherokee corn patches and stripped them clean of grain.

Even more exciting than Preacher Head was the remarkable and adventurous Christopher Columbus Graham. Abe idolized him. Born in 1787, on the banks of the Kentucky River, Christopher Graham had learned to shoot wolves and lynxes that attacked his father's calf pens by sticking a rifle through the cracks between the logs of the cabin. In time he was known as the best rifle shot on the frontier. He became a flatboatman and made twenty trips down the Kentucky, Ohio, and Mississippi rivers to New Orleans, bringing back strange tales and specimens of strange rocks, plants, animals, and fish. He was a friend of a young storekeeper in Elizabethtown named John James Audubon, who was also interested in the exciting world of nature around him, especially birds, and who took long canoe and walking trips, sometimes more than 1,000 miles distance. A flatboatman's life sounded exciting to Abe.

When the War of 1812 started, Christopher Graham left his studies at Transylvania College and visited his friend Tom Lincoln on Nolin Creek. Graham had just joined the

Kentucky volunteers to march off to the war. Nancy Lincoln and her children listened with grave concern as Tom and his friend debated whether or not Tom should go. Late in the night, Tom Lincoln banked the fire and said, "Nancy and the young'uns couldn't provide. I'll have to stay."

That night around the Lincoln fireside, Abe probably heard his hero, Christopher Graham, refer frequently to the man who would become the boy's second and lasting heroic idol, Mr. Henry Clay, Senator from Kentucky—The *Kentucky Gazette* had named him the "Western Star."

There were special heroes, Washington, Jefferson, and Henry Clay, but young Abe Lincoln also was fortunate because his world was a world of heroic men. Endurance, strength, conviction, adventure, and the frontier were one and inseparable.

And though far removed from the excitement of what was happening in the East and what had happened, the boy had kept Mr. Riney's word pictures of Washington and his men at Valley Forge. For Abe there was meaning to the apocryphal story of the boy Washington telling his father the truth about cutting down the cherry tree. Riding to the mill for a sack of cornmeal, Abe remembered Mr. Riney's story of Thomas Jefferson riding from Charlottesville, Virginia, to Washington for his inauguration as President, spending the night at Mrs. Brown's boardinghouse, and then walking alone over to the unfinished Capitol to be sworn in as President. "'All men are created equal,'" Mr. Riney had said.

CHAPTER FOUR

"Mr. Hazel Is Powerful Peculiar in Some of His Thinkin'"

M r. Riney had moved to greener pastures in a larger settlement, Pottinger's Creek, not far from Big Knob Lick (a village later renamed Rineyville in his honor).

On Knob Creek Abe and Sarah Lincoln began their second and last session of school in Kentucky. "Mr. Hazel will have a slateboard," Abe repeated several times to Sarah as they walked toward Caleb Hazel's house on the Athertonville road.

"He'll have a big slateboard. Don't fret so much," replied Sarah, " 'cause he's rich with real windows in his house. Ma said to be careful about settin' down cause there's storebought chairs in his house of smooth and shiny wood, and we darsn't scratch one. And I heard Pa tell Ma that there ain't no shuck ticks to sleep on in his house, nothing but feather ticks. Pa said too he heard that the injun, Mose, who works for Mr. Hazel, doesn't sleep in the wood shed like other injuns who work for white people. He sleeps in the house, Pa said, on a feather tick, just like Mr. Hazel and everybody else."

"I want to see an injun close up, don't you?" Abe called

back over his shoulder. All the reluctance which had held him back from Mr. Riney's school that first day, was gone. He was six steps ahead of Sarah and walking so fast she had a hard time keeping up.

"Ma says not to stare at the injun or act scairt. 'Cause he's an orphan and ain't harmful. Ma says Mr. Hazel found him at the forks of Salt River and Rolling Fork. That's why they call him Mose, after the Bible story. Don't get so fer ahead," Sarah called after Abe, whose linsey-woolsey breeches, the same ones he had worn to Mr. Riney's school, danced about his bare legs halfway between his knees and bare ankles.

Caleb Hazel kept a home school in his dwelling house which also doubled for an inn. He was related to the family of Nancy Hanks Lincoln by marriage and was a neighbor and friend of the Lincolns. One of his students simply remembered him as being "able to teach spelling, reading and indifferent writing—and perhaps could cipher to the rule of three" and was of sufficient size and bodily strength "to thrash any boy or youth that came to his school." He is also remembered as having been "a neat penman; a better than usual grammarian; and, generally, an outstanding scholar of that time and place, possessing, by frontier measurements, an excellent library."

Caleb Hazel had studied for a time under James Priestley at Priestley's school in Bardstown, known also as Salem Academy. Priestley had a statewide reputation as a teacher "who used the rod more than the quill." His school became one of the best known in the wilderness, numbering Benjamin and John J. Hardin, both outstanding lawyers, among its graduates. Five Kentucky counties were ultimately named for Priestley scholars.

45

"We'll probably see him first," Abe speculated as they came out of the woods and sighted the house by the side of the road near the far end of the clearing. "He'll be outside choppin' wood or sloppin' pigs or somethin', I reckon."

Abe slowed his pace as they approached the long, low log house——four times as long and twice as wide as the one where Abe and Sarah lived on Knob Creek.

They both knew Mr. Hazel as the tallest man in the whole county. They had seen him at both the South Fork and Little Mount churches were he was often the speakin' preacher when the Reverend John Bailey was away on the circuit. "It's got two chimneys," Sarah whispered, "and two doors. We'll knock at the near one." The hum of voices inside told them they were at the right part of the house. The hum also made it necessary for them to knock harder.

The door was opened by a boy about Abe's age and size, who in dress and looks could almost have been his twin, except that his leathery skin was a little darker than Abe's; he had a deep, withered groove of a scar that creased one cheek, beginning midway between his mouth and eye and ending just below the ear. Mr. Hazel waved Abe and Sarah in with his long pointing stick from where he stood at the front of the room. Inside there were nine or ten children, only about half the number that had been at Mr. Riney's school. Mr. Hazel welcomed Abe and Sarah and directed them to find places at the long puncheon benches which ran the length of the room. "Mr. Hazel's store-bought chairs must be in another room," Abe thought.

Abe sat down by the boy with the deep scar, and Sarah took a seat by one of Preacher Bailey's girls. Abe recognized the Kirkpatrick children who lived in a stone house, "one of the best houses in the county," his father had often told

46

him as they passed it on their way to Hodgen's Mill. Abe
didn't see his friend Austin Gallaher or the Duncans, but
the Brownlees and Ashcrofts from Mr. Riney's school were
there.

"You missed the Scripture reading." Mr. Hazel spoke in
a soft voice which seemed out of place coming from the
great frame which almost reached the log-beamed loft ceil-
ing of the room. "But it's the best Scripture for a school's
beginning, so we'll have it again tomorrow.

"How far can you spell and read?" Mr. Hazel asked
Sarah as he pointed to the speller, held together with
moccasin-stitching, which Sarah held proudly in front of
her.

"Most all with some stumbling toward the back." Sarah was pleased to speak out.

"And how about you?" Mr. Hazel asked as he turned to Abe.

"Same as Sarah, I reckon, but I can write better'n her. That's what Pa says." And all the while Abe's eyes stayed fixed on the slateboard which hung against the wall at the front of the room. The writing at the top of the slate puzzled Abe. The first line said: "Lodging 3 cents"; below that, "Half pint of whiskey 6 cents"; and finally, "Stabling and Hay 6 cents."

The puzzle was cleared up when the writing exercises were over at the end of the day. Mr. Hazel took the slateboard down and hung it outside the far door of his long house. "Them's the inn fares," the boy with the deep scar told Abe as they stood together at the front of the building.

A quizzical look reflected the questions which were buzzing inside Abe's head. Just at the end of school Mr. Hazel had read an advertisement from the *Kentucky Gazette*. The ad had quickened Abe's heartbeat: "Mr. William Leavy's Emporium has just received from Philadelphia a large supply of school and family slates: Framed, 10 x 12 inches, 5 cents; 12 x 16 inches, 8 cents." Mr. Hazel explained that if parents could pay either of these amounts as the first supplies subscription, he would order the slates from Lexington. Abe had looked across the room at Sarah and nodded his head up and down—"Yes, Pa will." But Sarah, after much hesitation, had moved her head slowly from side to side—"I don't know. I doubt if he can."

But Abe had another question. He seemed to be trying to see around both sides of the house at once. Some of the children were well along the road in the direction of their cabins. Sarah stood in the road motioning for Abe to come on. "Have you seen that injun that lives here?" Abe finally asked the boy with the scar on his cheek.

"I'm who he is," the boy replied with a smile, "but my name ain't Mose. Folks just call me that 'cause Mr. Hazel saved me from scalp hunters when they shot my Ma and Pa on the raft we was movin' on where Rollin' Fork runs into the Salt River. My name is Mourning Dove 'cause my Pa said when I was born I wailed deep and long like a dove."

Abe moved a step closer and was about to ask "How'd you get that scar?" but changed his mind. "Sarah's motionin', I've got to go. I'll call you by your real name tomorrow. Is Mr. Hazel gonna buy you one of them slates?"

"I reckon he might," the boy called after Abe as he hurried to catch up with Sarah.

There had been much about the first day at Mr. Hazel's school which was "powerful puzzlin'" to both Abe and Sarah. "Laura Brownlee says there ain't no more children comin' to the school," Sarah said when Abe had caught up with her. "She says their folks don't like Mr. Hazel, call him names just because of Mose. Said a lot of people wanted to raid his house and scalp the Mose when they heard that Mr. Hazel had driven off scalp hunters who killed the boy's Pa and Ma and saved him when he was floatin' on a raft, shiverin' and bleedin', hunkered down between his dead Ma and Pa."

"I thought he was a big injun. The kind I dream about hidin' behind the corn shocks. But he's just a boy like me: I called him Mose, but that ain't his name, and he didn't get mad. He's got a real injun name, Mourning Dove. He don't look like no injun. He ain't much darker than the Cassnas children who were at Mr. Riney's school. And dressed like me I couldn't tell the difference. I'm gonna set on the bench with him 'cause he's got a speller and a geography book all his own."

"Bet he won't let you look at 'em," Sarah volunteered.

"Has already," replied Abe.

"Don't talk so much," Sarah said quietly. "When I'm walkin' in the woods, I like to be able to hear if there are any varmints. Pa and Ma didn't tell us about Mr. Hazel the way they did Mr. Riney. I wonder why? I'm gonna ask 'em. I heard 'em whispering about him one night, and Ma said he'd be a fine teacher, and it was better not to take sides. A home-based teacher, she said, he'll be a good'n."

When Sarah and Abe came into the clearing of their Knob Creek farm, their father was working in the corn patch. Abe waved and kept going, headed straight for the cabin. He would tell his Pa about Mose and school later. Right now a store-bought slate from Leavy's Emporium was uppermost in his mind, and he knew that the place to start if he would get it was with his Ma. At the age of seven Abe was already aware of the demands of the wilderness, described around cabin firesides as "takin' a lot of calculatin'."

Between chores Abe talked to his Ma. He brought a bucket of water from the spring. He drove the shoats from the woods and penned them "against the varmints." He penned the cow in the corner of the lot for his mother to milk. And by the time Nancy Lincoln had finished milking Abe was "pretty sure" that he and Sarah were going to share one of Leavy's five-cent slates between them. "The small

50

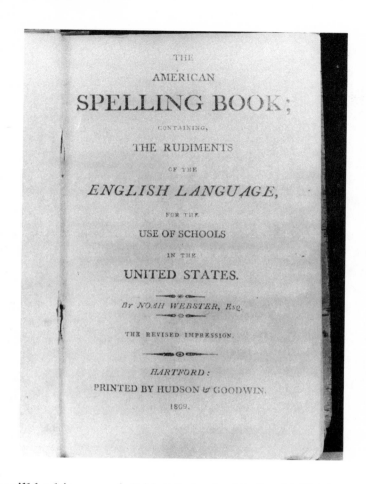

THE

AMERICAN

SPELLING BOOK;

CONTAINING,

THE RUDIMENTS

OF THE

ENGLISH LANGUAGE,

FOR THE

USE OF SCHOOLS

IN THE

UNITED STATES.

By NOAH WEBSTER, Esq.

THE REVISED IMPRESSION.

HARTFORD:

PRINTED BY HUDSON & GOODWIN.

1809.

one will be big enough," his Ma had said, "and it'll be easier to carry and not so much danger of breakin'.""

So when Tom Lincoln came from the corn patch at dusk, Abe had already started a fire to "take off the damp chill." He stretched his bony frame on the hearth, doing his words from the old moccasin-sewed speller and feeling warm inside and out.

"I reckon it's all right," Tom Lincoln had said. "I still have the wolf scalps from last winter to collect the bounty on from the county clerk in Elizabethtown. There's more nubbins than we need for meal to sell to Hodgen at the mill when I get time to fetch 'em to him. We'll be in pretty good shape if I git my lawsuit settled over the title of the Nolin Creek land and git a fair price."

Now it was Sarah's turn at last, for she hadn't been able to get a "word in edgeways." "Laura Brownlee says people was gonna raid Mr. Hazel's house and scalp Mose. Why? He ain't no varmint. Abe set with him in school. He's a boy like Abe. Abe was scairt when we got to school, thought he'd be big and outside choppin' or sumthin'. But he was inside learnin'; calls writin' and figurin' bird tracks."

"That's why some ain't sendin' their young'uns, I reckon," Pa replied. "It's all right to have an injun who's hired or has bartered himself for debt, if he sleeps in the shed and eats at the outside bench. But in the house— treated respectable—most people don't take kindly to that. People always says they carry lice and ticks and spread the pox. People don't see much cause for Mose to learn readin', writin', and cipherin'. Everybody thinks his own way. But times has changed a lot since your grandpa was killed by Indians at the edge of his clearing. Kentucky don't pay scalp bounties no more, but some people do. There ain't many people who feel like Mr. Hazel feels except preachers. Mr. Hazel's powerful peculiar in some of this thinkin', but he's an educated man and can teach you sumthin'."

When the children began their second day of school, Sarah took her seat on the puncheon bench by Laura Brownlee and Abe sat by his new friend, Mourning Dove.

"As I said yesterday," Mr. Hazel began, "book learning is no good if a person doesn't get soul learning along with it. And what was our soul learning about yesterday?"

" 'Bout a parcel of people who didn't like what Jesus was teachin'," came back in a chorus with a broken cadence, "and they got a lawyer and tried to snare Him in an argument."

"What did they put the lawyer up to ask Him?" This time Mr. Hazel pointed his long stick at Abe, who was looking sideways at Mourning Dove's geography book.

"I don't know," Abe replied with a quiver in his voice.

"We wasn't here for the Scripture lesson yesterday," Sarah said, coming quickly to her brother's aid.

"I'm sorry, I forgot," said Mr. Hazel, as he swung his stick and pointed to Mourning Dove for an answer.

"The lawyer asked Him what is the greatest commandment in the law," answered Mourning Dove without hesitation.

"And what did Jesus answer?" asked Mr. Hazel as he swung his rod over the whole group, for this meant everybody could answer.

"To love God with all your heart, and with all your soul, and with all your mind," replied the chorus, losing a few voices toward the end.

"Now," said Mr. Hazel opening his Bible, "I will read the most important part of the lesson. The part that we want to remember. This is the first and great commandment. And the second is like unto it. 'Thou shalt love thy neighbor as thyself.' "

"Is your neighbor only the person who lives in the next clearing?" Mr. Hazel pointed his rod at Naomi Bailey.

"Jesus meant your neighbor is everybody," Naomi replied.

"Now this is our lesson," began Mr. Hazel, waving his rod in a wide arch, "and what does it mean in Knob Creek and Athertonville, and Kentucky and Virginia?"

"It means to treat everybody the way you want them to treat you." And the loud response rattled the real glass in Mr. Hazel's windows.

"Does everybody include only white men?" Mr. Hazel asked slowly.

"The people at Pa's church say it includes slaves, too," Naomi Bailey volunteered as she blushed red, looking from side to side as though she wished only Mr. Hazel had heard her.

Some days it was hard to tell when soul learning ended and book learning began at Mr. Hazel's school. It was equally difficult to sort out home learning and school learning. All intertwined to meet the demands of life in a frontier community. At many firesides children learned, as Naomi Bailey had, that the black man in slavery was wrongly treated as a beast of burden and sold as horses and cows at auctions. At fewer firesides, few indeed, some children doubtless listened with mixed emotions when a case was made for the Indian.

Abe's impressionable years in Kentucky were haunted by fear of lurking savages. Mothers disciplined their children with the household phrase "Indians carry off bad boys and girls." But there were really very few Indians left in Abe's Kentucky. A few Choctaw, Shawnee, and Cherokee lived away from the white man and tended their own corn patches. But they too lived in fear. While Kentucky was still

54

a part of Virginia, a kind governor might provide funds to pay a bounty for Indian scalps. After Kentucky became a state in 1795, scalp hunters were paid by popular subscription collected on county or local basis.

This had been the fate of Mourning Dove's parents. As young Abe heard the story at Caleb Hazel's school, Little Duck, Mourning Dove's father, living in fear of the white man, had decided to leave his corn patch on the upper Rolling Fork and move west. With his wife and child, he started the journey by raft down Rolling Fork. Rolling Fork emptied into the Salt River, and the Salt River into the Ohio, the great water highway west. Little Duck had journeyed only as far as the mouth of Rolling Fork when he was ambushed by scalp hunters. Caleb Hazel, returning from Louisville, had surprised the scalp hunters and driven them off with his flintlock. When the raft drifted ashore, he found an Indian child crouching between the dead bodies of his father and mother. Blood smeared his face where a bullet had torn away part of his cheek. This was Mourning Dove, at the time not more than five or six years old. Now some of the settlers had talked of "scalping and burning out that injun lover Hazel."

But Caleb Hazel and his father could not be frightened. With the help of a few settlers who thought as they thought and the eloquent and inspiring voice of the Reverend David Rice, they drove Indian bounty hunters from Kentucky. "However degraded and savage you may think the Indian," cried the Reverend David Rice, "there is no degradation and savagery so base as that of a man who makes his living by murdering another man and selling his scalp for the same price he gets for the head of a timber wolf."

55

Caleb Hazel told his pupils stories of this remarkable and tireless missionary of the wilderness, as teachers of all time have placed before their pupils the lives of those whom they might one day, grown to manhood, seek to emulate. Educated at Hampden-Sydney College in Virginia, the Reverend David Rice had carried the Gospel and advanced the cause of freedom in the wilderness for forty years. Among the Indians in the wilds of what later became West Virginia, he was called the "messiah of the Monongahela." As a member of the convention to draw up a state constitution for Kentucky he had cried out against slavery: "Holding men in slavery is a national vice in Virginia, and while a part of that state, we were partakers of the guilt. As a separate state we are just now come to the birth; and it depends on our free choice whether we shall be born in this sin, or remain innocent of it by acknowledging, what has been written but not practiced, 'that all men are created free and equal.'"

As the "father of Presbyterianism in the West," David Rice had worked for the church to take a stand against slavery without dividing the church itself, that it might be done in such a manner as to not "disturb the peace of Zion." There were 1,238 slaves listed as property in Hardin County the year that Abe was attending Caleb Hazel's school. Besides the soul learning at school, there was talk at home. Tom and Nancy Lincoln talked with their friends about the split in the South Fork Baptist Church. Fifteen members, "holding that we cannot join in Christian fellowship with those who assert the right of perpetual slavery," had left and formed the Little Mount Anti-Slavery Church. This was the church which Tom and Nancy Lincoln at-

56

tended. It was here too that Abe's little brother, Thomas, was buried.

Perhaps young Abe learned also at home or school that Mr. Hazel, believing, like his mentor and friend the Reverend Mr. Rice, that the "peace of Zion" must not be disturbed, did not withdraw. Did he say to his friends or his pupils, "The house of our Lord divided against itself is contrary to His teachings; there must be a better way"? Caleb Hazel attended both churches, scorned by some at each, perhaps appreciated by few.

Abe and Sarah walked to and from Mr. Hazel's school, learning by rote, learning by pondering, and learning by being. The treasured, small slate came at last from Leavy's Emporium, and he and Sarah took turns writing their words and ciphering on it.

In school he heard older pupils read from *The Kentucky Preceptor*, a collection of history, poems, essays, and Scripture. It contained a debate entitled "Which has the Most to Complain of, the Indian, or the Negro?" He heard the older pupils read it in class. It stirred him up inside. His hero, Christopher Graham, had shot Indians. Indians had killed his grandpa. But now there was his friend, Mourning Dove, and there was Mr. Hazel.

Chasing a skittish heifer in the woods, he sometimes felt that not to be able to run would be like slavery. Helping his Pa dig in the corn patch, he felt the great joy of freedom to lay down his hoe and walk to the cabin for a gourd dipper of cool water. Preacher Bailey believed like Mr. Hazel's friend, Preacher Rice, that all men are created equal. But Preacher Hodge said that "God put a mark on Cain, when he killed his brother Abel, so that men would know him

57

and treat him accordingly. The mark was that God made him black, and meant for him to be punished forever. That's why he and his people are slaves, and that's what God intended."

What was a boy to believe? When Abe took his puzzlin' questions to his Pa, Tom Lincoln would reply, "Thar's sum that thinks one way and sum a'tother." When he asked his Ma who was right, Preacher Bailey or Preacher Hodge, she would ponder a long time and say, "I reckon only the Lord knows."

Preacher Bailey said: "Ole Pharaoh's country was cursed with plagues. The rivers turned to blood; the sand turned to lice. Locusts ate up the corn patches, and the angel of death struck down the oldest boy in every family. All because ole Pharaoh wouldn't listen to Moses and free the slaves, and they'd already been slaves for four hundred years. I hope the Lord never sends down a visitation on Kentucky and the United States of America. But when swarms of passenger pigeons eats the corn in the patch, when a mad timber wolf bites a shoat and give it lockjaw, and it spreads among all the critters and they die, ain't these the same signs that God gave ole Pharaoh? When the milk sickness hits and carries off our wimmen and young'uns, ain't that a warnin' that God's gonna one day send down a Moses if we don't raise up one?"

Sometimes on the bench outside the cabin or by the fireside there was deep talk: "How fur away the stars look tonight. It's hard to understand when a youngun jus' borned is took." Tom Lincoln would say, "I reckon livin' is mighty puzzlin'." Abe would look at the stars or the shadows that the flames from the fire changed into strange shapes on the walls of the cabin and agree with his Pa. Sometimes after a long quiet Abe would tell his Pa about the book Mr. Hazel had with "a picture of the whole world that somebody had drawed."

For at Caleb Hazel's school Abe saw his first geography books. Hazel had somewhere acquired copies of both Jedidiah Morse's *Geography Made Easy* and O'Neill's *Geography*. Morse, a graduate of Yale, the father of Samuel F. B., who was the inventor of the telegraph, published his geography in 1789. Maps were inaccurate and few in number. The book was really a universal history as seen through the eyes of Morse, who was also a theologian and temperance crusader. Instruction was by question and answer. In answer to a question regarding New England exports the author added his comments on New England rum. "It is not," he said, "a wholesome liquor. It has killed more Indians than their wars and sicknesses. It does not spare white people, especially when made into flip, which is rum mixed with small beer, and muscovado sugar." It followed, of course, that the next question was: "What is muscovado sugar?" Answer: "Muscovado sugar is the dark raw sugar that remains after the molasses has been extracted from the juice of the sugar cane."

O'Neill's *Geography* was a larger book, containing 386 pages. It contained maps of the Eastern and Western Hemispheres and a very inaccurate map of the eastern half of the United States. The last 64 pages of the book introduced the scholar to astronomy. Instruction here was also by question and answer.

59

Q. What do you observe worthy of particular remark relative to Asia?

A. This grand division of the earth is particularly remarkable, as being the theatre of almost every action recorded in the Holy Scriptures. For in it the Almighty planted the Garden of Eden, in which he formed our first and common parents, Adam and Eve, from whom the whole race of mankind has descended. Asia, after the Deluge, became again the nursery of the world, whence the descendents of Noah dispersed their various colonies into all other parts of the globe.

Abe went back for a second reading, perhaps for a third and fourth. For Abe and his contemporaries, passages such as this contained mystery and meaning worthy of memorization.

Lincoln later recalled that "Because we had so little to learn from that we chewed over everything many times. And when we heard something at school that we thought our parents hadn't heard, we could hardly wait to get home and tell it to them."

The school session with Mr. Hazel ended for Abe and Sarah. The excitement of school was replaced by the excitement of moving. Disputed land titles continued to plague the Kentucky settlers. So Tom Lincoln had decided to move to Indiana after the "crops was gathered." The dream of a new home, the thrill of seeing the mighty Ohio River, filled young Abe's mind. He was not yet eight years old. Momentarily Mr. Riney and Mr. Hazel faded into the background of childhood memories.

CHAPTER FIVE

"*It Was a Wild Region*"

Tom Lincoln had grown to manhood as a farmhand in Kentucky and Indiana and a boatman on the mighty Ohio River. His deep hazel eyes had seen more of the country than most of his neighbors and acquaintances. He had made at least one trip down the Ohio and the "Father of Waters," as the Indians called the muddy and mysterious Mississippi, to New Orleans. Having reached manhood, he had become a skilled carpenter and cabinetmaker, bought a 238-acre farm, and had served as a juryman, a member of the county patrol, and a road supervisor—all before he was twenty-three years old. By the time Abe was born in 1809 his father was the fifteenth highest taxpayer on the Hardin County tax list. He owned two farms totaling 586½ acres, two town lots in Elizabethtown, the county seat, and was taxed for four horses at a time when one horse was average for a frontier farmer.

In the early autumn of 1816 the former riverman Thomas Lincoln built a flatboat near the Rolling Fork Creek. He loaded the boat with 400 gallons of whiskey (then, as now, one of Kentucky's most salable products) and started for the mighty Ohio. He was preparing to leave

61

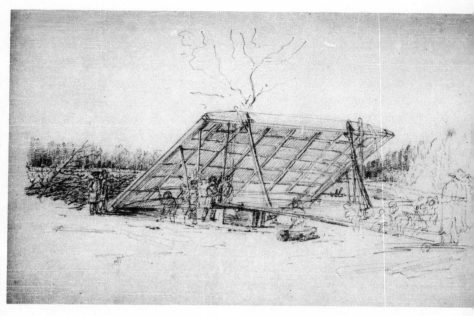

Kentucky for reasons other than the "eternal call" to the frontiersman. Land titles in Kentucky were difficult. Many land warrants had been issued without surveys while the territory was part of Virginia. Thomas Lincoln had discovered that the deed to his Knob Creek farm was imperfect. Lawsuits claiming title to several Knob Creek valley farms were filed against Lincoln and his neighbors.

A hundred miles west, in the Indiana Territory, land was being carefully surveyed by the government, and a young Congressional delegate from the territory named William Henry Harrison had persuaded lawmakers in Washington to enact the "quarter section-two dollar an acre" law. So Thomas Lincoln sold his Knob Creek farm at a loss, leaving the new owner to complete the fight for title, and prepared to move across the Ohio River to Indiana.

The journey "to spy out the land" was made alone. Thomas Lincoln's brother Josiah had already moved to Harrison County, Indiana, and Tom Lincoln was also acquainted with one Thomas Carter, who had settled on Little Pigeon Creek, 18 miles inland from the west bank ferry landing at the mouth of Anderson's Creek. Leaving his whiskey (to be converted into money later) with a man named Francis Posey at Thompson's Ferry on the west bank of the Ohio, Tom Lincoln found his way to Little Pigeon Creek and staked out a "quarter section," 160 acres, in southern Indiana's vast and overwhelming forest.

Having blazed trees and piled brush on the corners of his 160 acres, Tom Lincoln hurried back to Knob Creek. An auction had to be held to dispose of surplus personal property. Two horses, one or two cows, small pigs (hogs were plentiful), cooking utensils, ticks and coverlets for beds, clothing, and other personal effects doubtless constituted the goods carried into Indiana. Tom Lincoln's tools had already been taken on the flatboat. He would make furniture after a cabin was built.

Holding on to the pole railing of the ferry that carried him across the Ohio to Indiana, Abe searched in vain for the bottom of the river and wondered if he would ever be as good a riverman as his father.

Abe's father thought that being a flatboatman was a good idea, but Abe's mother and Sarah were not so sure; they felt "lots safer" when the ferry edged up against land and they stood in Indiana.

"Snow would fly" before a cabin was ready unless Tom Lincoln moved rapidly, and there is no evidence to indicate that the Lincoln family was not well settled by about the date that Indiana became a state, December 11, 1816.

Carrying and driving the essential chattels for frontier existence, the family travelled through the wooded hills of southern Indiana toward Pigeon Creek and their 160 acres of virgin soil. In typical frontier style the family settled there and lived through some "pretty pinching times," as was the lot of most on the frontier.

Working with the aid of a few neighbors (a frontier custom always provided volunteer help to the new settler), Tom Lincoln probably had the largest cabin the Lincolns had ever lived in, 14 feet by 20, with a loft, ready before the snow began to fly.

Although Dennis Hanks, who arrived in Indiana a year later with Nancy Hanks' aunt and uncle, Betsy and Thomas Sparrow, said that the Lincolns lived the first winter in a lean-to, there is evidence to the contrary from Abraham Lincoln himself.

He recalled that "a few days before the completion of his eighth year, in the absence of his father, a flock of wild turkeys approached the new log cabin, and A. with a rifle gun, standing inside, shot through a crack, and killed one of them. He has never since pulled a trigger on any larger game."

Sarah Hawley, accustomed to the spacious farmhouses of Connecticut, spent a year as a frontier doctor in the Ohio Valley, 1820–21. In *A Journal of a Tour*, published in 1822, he left an unforgettable picture of these "pinching times":

In riding through the country, you come to a log or block house (a block house was built of logs hewn on two sides); on enquiring to whom it belongs, you are surprised to hear that it belongs to Judge _____. The whole establishment consists of one room, in which all the family, with their guests, eat, sleep, and perform all the domestic operations. You proceed a little farther, and arrive at a similar mansion, and are informed that it belongs to Esquire _____, who you find is a miller. . . .

Soliciting information respecting another residence, you are told that it is the property of a Representative or a Senator of the Legislature of the State. . . . In this villa, containing also but one room, is found a bed in two corners, in another a cup-board, in the fourth a swill-barrel. . . .

The furniture of most houses is scanty. Few families have more than one indifferent table, and chairs of the plainest kind, and most of them either broken or worn out, just sufficient to accommodate the family; so that, should company call to see them, the guests or some part of the family must either stand, or sit on the bed, or some stool or block of wood which is more convenient.

The furniture for the table is equally scanty and inconvenient. I once had occasion to dine with a family —where six of us set (*sic*) at the table. There was a plate for each of us, a large dish in the middle of the table contained the food. I had the good fortune to obtain a decent knife and fork, one of the family had a shoe-knife and a fork, another (if I mistake not) an old raisor-blade (*sic*) with a wooden handle, and the other three were content with forks only.

Similar descriptions from eyewitnesses can be multiplied to show the near equality of economic and social conditions which made the frontier "the great leveler." The lives of young and old, the more learned and the less learned, were brought together by the "compulsive restrictions" of the small neighborhood. Each member was conscious of a dependence on their neighbors, yet, at the same time, each possessed a proud sense of self-sufficiency and self-confidence. These two factors created independence, self-respect, and a "general tolerance of the opinions and manners of others." Although the legend of his rise to greatness has demanded that Lincoln began in surroundings inferior to those of his neighbors, there are no facts to substantiate any great difference.

CHAPTER SIX

"Nothing to Excite Ambition for Education"

In the general area of Little Pigeon Creek where Thomas Lincoln settled with his family in 1816 there were only about seven families—not enough to support a teacher. And there would not be enough children to provide one until the fall of 1819. It was during these years that Lincoln, perhaps without any awareness of future value to him, began consciously practicing total attentiveness, the art of listening.

An infant listens through wonder and the desire for security. The world is full of new sounds. Slowly some sounds take on an association. A soft word, a name repeated draws a line around the limitless wonder, and, close within the center of familiarity the child listens and feels secure.

The second stage of listening grows out of admiration and expresses itself in imitation. Imitation, for most people, remains standard as they grow into adulthood, and for many, imitative listening loses much of the accuracy that admiration had demanded in childhood.

Few people ever achieve the third stage of listening, creative listening. This is the quality that adds clarity, depth, and compassion to what is heard.

The frontier, where life gave no quarter and demanded much, was conducive to that intuitive learning which demands above-average use of the senses. William H. Herndon in researching his biography of Lincoln asked Dennis Hanks, a cousin and contemporary of Lincoln, how Lincoln and Hanks had learned so much in Indiana under such disadvantages. "We learned by sight, scent, and hear-

DENNIS HANKS

ing," said Hanks. "We heard all that was said and talked over and over the questions heard, wore them slick, greasy and threadbare." Hanks also recalled that "Abe was a good listener to his superiors, bad to his inferiors. He couldn't stand idle jabber."

Abe Lincoln and Dennis Hanks, growing up together in the wilderness where there was "nothing to excite ambition for education," are symbolic of the riddle of education. They began about the same, with the same chances. One fed his soul hunger; the other was content "to live by bread alone."

To develop fully the art of listening—listening with "the third ear"—there must be a sufficient amount of silence. The Indiana wilderness provided this silence. Outside the cabin there was intensive listening to interpret the changing mood of the wind in giant oaks—"Was it brewing a storm?" There was the inquiring silence which stilled the clearing after the "hello" of the stranger from its edge— "Does he come friendly? Does he bring good news or bad?" In the long silence when the far off riflelike crack of an ax on wood ceased there was measured listening—"Too long for a blow" (the frontiersman's term for a rest period). "Did he cut himself, the tree didn't fall? Are wolves there?"

Inside the cabin there was, of course, jabber and talk of the dull routine and everyday things. But there was more. There was gentle talk of ways and means to "live out the winter." There was secondhand news from the Louisville papers. There were stories of what was happening "back East," told by the stranger, taken in for the night. There was good news of a new mill on Pigeon Creek or a store being opened at Gentryville. There was sad news of wolves ravaging a neighbor's pigs or of ague, cold plague, or milk sickness "in the holler" on the other side of French Lick. These were things to hear, to listen to with total attention. Tomorrow the listener would pass on message and meaning to a neighbor—be it pleasant and reassuring or ominous.

Abe later recalled that he would go to his bedroom, "after hearing the neighbors talk of an evening with my father, and spend no small part of the night walking up and down trying to make out what was the exact meaning of some of their, to me, dark sayings.

"I could not sleep, although I tried to, when I went on such a hunt for an idea, until I had caught it; and when I thought I had got it, I was not satisfied until I had put it in language plain enough, as I thought, for any boy I knew to comprehend. This was a kind of passion with me, and it has stuck by me; for I am never easy now, when I am handling a thought, till I have bounded it north, bounded it south, and bounded it east, and bounded it west."

Lincoln said that "when a mere child, I used to get irritated when anybody talked to me in a way I could not understand. I do not think I ever got angry at anything else in my life; but that has always disturbed my temper, and has ever since."

His stepmother, Sarah Bush Lincoln, described Abe's listening to Jesse Weik about eight months after Lincoln's assassination, and was quoted in his book *The Real Lincoln* as saying: "I remember that when neighbors came to set Abe was a silent and listening child. He never spoke or asked anything until they were gone. And then he had to understand everything, even the smallest thing that I often hadn't heard. When he understood he would repeat it over and over again, sometimes in one form and then in another. When it was fixed in his mind to suit him he stopped frettin' and he never lost that fact or his understanding of it. Sometimes he seemed pestered to give expression to his views and got mad almost at anyone who couldn't explain plainly what he wanted to convey."

This was no indifferent imitative listening that would have merely lulled a boy to sleep, leaving a garbled message to be repeated in fragmentary distortions, if at all. This was not the type of classroom listening that asks only parrotlike recall.

Of this behavior Dr. C. Alphonso Smith wrote: "It is this passion for self-expression that made Lincoln one of the great spokesmen of his age. It enabled him to say in many letters and speeches what others were beginning to feel but could not express. It made him one of the great masters of English prose. He became a leader of men because he interpreted them to themselves. He gave back as rain what he received as mist."

Gangly and awkward, Abe teetered on a slippery rock at the edge of Little Pigeon Creek. He did not hear his mother calling. "Abe, It's milkin' time. Fetch the cows from the thicket." He was watching a great snowy owl perched on a rock, fishing in the stream with one claw. He had heard the neighbors talk of signs and omens: "When an owl feeds in the daylight, trouble will come in the night." His mother called again: "Abe, Abe, why don't you bring home the cows?" He didn't hear her; he was listening to the pulse of the earth beating upon his ears. And his mother called, "Abe, fetch the cows." The dull clank of the cow bell drifted over the clearing to Nancy Hanks Lincoln, but her boy didn't answer.

71

CHAPTER SEVEN

"*There I Grew Up*"

With calloused toes gripping a slippery rock and a September day faltering as the sun dropped slowly— quarter, half, three-quarters—below the wall of beech, oak, and sycamore, there was much to detain a nine-year-old boy at cowtime. But out of the thicket at last came the lead cow with the bell. Skittish heifers and last spring's calves, followed, slowed by three or four half-grown hogs. Abe was behind. Now and then he got close enough to clout the sleek side of a shoat with the black alder sapling he'd used as a fishing pole a few minutes earlier.

Abe was growing up after the pattern of other frontier children. Perhaps he heard the silence of the wilderness more keenly. Perhaps he remembered and pondered the ill omen of the "owl feeding in daylight" with more interest than average. But it was not noticeable. And he had failed to hear his mother's call, as boys and girls the world over, before and after him, fail to hear their mother's call when it is "chore time."

He saw his father's ax strike deep in the tree at the edge of the clearing, but the sound came to him later over the tasseled corn—"sight travels faster than sound," he said.

Abe learned that standing at a particular spot in the valley near the salt lick, he could call his name and it would come back to him in an echo. Sarah said it was a "haunt" calling his name, that the whole world was full of "haunts." The world was full—full of mysteries. If when he "hollered out" his name, it went over the ridge instead of hitting it and bouncing back, where would it stop?

For three days a deer came to the lick with her fawn. And then she came alone. Abe followed her, deeper and deeper into the woods, demanding total recall of his memory. This crooked tree, this bittersweet vine, this bent spice bush—all must be remembered or he would lose his way back to the salt lick and the clearing.

He watched the doe paw the ground and smell where she pawed. Abe slipped from tree to tree, closer and closer.

The doe was not pawing the earth after all. She was trying to awaken her fawn. The fawn did not move. It was dead, its insides eaten out. The doe caught the scent of the boy. She ran away.

That night in the cabin Sarah said, "The doe will come back to try to wake her fawn again."

Abe said, "She never will."

"Creatures know more than we think they do." his Pa said quietly.

"If the varmints had killed the mother, it would have been worse," said his mother. "The fawn would have been left to die some way. There's good and bad in everything it seems like."

Sarah asked, "Is there a heaven where dead fawns go?" No one tried to answer. Abe was busy making his memory hold all the sayings of his father and mother.

His world demanded instant memorization. Back in Kentucky Mr. Riney had said, "You can't take the books home, and there's no slate big enough to copy all you want to know. So if you want to know it, you have to remember it." Abe's Indiana world up until this time, almost devoid of books and writing material, had provided for him a practice field for memorization which would equip him with memory and recall powers scarcely believable.

It was about this time that Abe attended court for the first time. The store, the mill, and the court were the social and political centers for the men and boys of the frontier. So Thomas Lincoln, having heard talk of a fiery young prosecuting attorney named John A. Brackenridge, rode horseback with Abe behind him to Boonville, 12 miles from Pigeon Creek, to spend a day at court.

Nearly fifty years later John A. Brackenridge visited his son, George, who had been given a post in the Treasury Department in Washington. The elder Brackenridge called on President Lincoln. Lincoln, his mind beset by a thousand problems, his spirit anguished in the midst of a terrible war, described the day in Boonville fifty years before. He recalled the names of the accused, recited part of Brackenridge's cross-examination of witnesses and his summary of the case to the jury. The elder Brackenridge, marveling at such power of memory, repeated the story many times before his death a few years after Lincoln's assassination.

If Abe had known he could read an account of the trial in a newspaper the next day, he might have required less than total imprint of his memory. Outward disadvantage, lack of learning aids and tools, remained a disadvantage and an excuse for many of Abe's contemporaries, but some turned it into an inward advantage—the advantage of becoming aware of what they could demand of their minds.

Here in the Buckhorn Valley of Spencer County, Indiana, Lincoln's childhood, like all childhoods, was made up of beginnings, some easily understood as natural and in "due course of time." Others seemed unnatural and apart from the way things should happen. These were the inevitable lessons of life, accepted as "bound to happen," but not easily understood.

In a hundred frontier settlements, in a thousand wilderness cabins, people like Tom Lincoln and his family were those of whom it was said: "Only the brave started and the weak died on the way."

There were good huskin' days and bad huskin' days; good crop seasons and bad crop seasons; years that were "mighty favorable" and years that were lean; times when nature was "powerful contrary" and acorns were few, and corn ears were nubbins, and meat and cornbread became "fearfulsum precious."

Families came to grips with the vexin' problems of living and learned that "nature knows her ways" but sometimes leaves man "powerful puzzled." And dreaming by a log fire or scanning a dark imprisoning horizon, Tom Lincoln and his neighbors found a single answer, "What will be will be," for "the earth is the Lord's."

"Bad news and plague travel on the wind" was a frontier saying. And so it was with the wind which blew over the Ohio past Posey's Landing, over the yellow poplars, brown oaks, and reddening maples in late September, 1818. Word came to Pigeon Creek that the dreaded "milk sick" was killing cows and people as it moved from settlement to settlement.

"Milk sick" was one of the frontier plagues, like "bilious spell," "cold plague," and "ague," which thrived on the unsanitary conditions prevalent in every cabin. The "milk sick" itself usually struck among the milk cows first. The cows got the disease from eating white snakeroot, a poisonous plant. The poison remained in the milk and was contracted by those drinking it, especially women. It began with a "coated tongue" followed by "chills and fever," which lasted for a period of from five to seven days. The victim would grow weaker and weaker with each passing day. Sometime between the fifth and seventh day the "fever broke," and the victim slowly recovered. If the fever did not "break," the sufferer died.

By October 5, 1818, the Pigeon Creek settlement lived

in grief and stark fear. More than a dozen cows had died, as had Betsy and Thomas Sparrow, with whom Dennis Hanks made his home. Dead also were Levi and Nancy Hall and Peter Brooner's wife. To nine-year-old Abe and Sarah, almost thirteen, the grimness was real indeed. Their mother had been sick for six days.

One of the neighbors, William Wood, had "set up" with Tom Lincoln through the night, watching over the thirty-six-year-old mother "too poorly" to turn herself under the heavy quilted "kivver." "The fever oughta break before long," said Wood as he left to return to his own cabin. "If you need me, I'll be over yander," he said. Avoiding Tom Lincoln's eyes, Wood nodded in the direction of his own cabin.

"She's powerful weak," said Tom Lincoln. "Powerful weak."

Sarah and Abe went to milk the two cows left alive. Abe drove them over the stubble patch where the corn stood in shocks, and put them through the bar-way to nibble at frosted grass and the yellow and crimson leaves of alder and sassafras saplings in the thicket. He pulled six stalks of fodder from the nearest corn shock and threw it over the rails to the cows. He was a long time getting back to the cabin because he counted the rows of stubble along the way—there had been no rows missed in the planting. He spoke quietly to himself: "Ma will be all right." He stopped and stood in the bright October sun. It was warm on his face and neck. When at last he stopped by the split log that doubled for step and bench at the door of the cabin, Sarah came out with a wooden bucket and said, "Go fetch some water."

There were leaves of all colors strewn along the path that led down the hill to the spring. The brightest were dogwood and sumac. He picked up a brilliant red dogwood leaf, twirled it between his fingers, and then began to chew on the stem. His Ma had told him to "never chew sumac, it's poison."

When he brought the water, Thomas Lincoln sent him out of the cabin to gather the "shaven" under the bucksaw rack and the sawhorse near the woodpile where Tom Lincoln and his neighbors had made coffins for Mrs. Brooner, the Sparrows, and the Halls. Abe had the crude deerskin sack almost full when his father came out of the cabin and crossed the few yards that separated the woodpile from the house. Abe had knocked one end of a half-whipsawed log about six feet long off the sawhorse. His father put it back.

"Abe, your Ma is dead. Will you go and ask Mr. Wood if he can kum for a spell? And then go and see if Mr. Brooner can kum."

He started toward the cabin door dragging the deerskin sack of shavings. He let them drop when he saw Sarah standing in the door. Her eyes were on the edge of the clearing as though she saw someone coming. She came out and went to the back of the cabin. Abe followed her. He thought he heard somebody call "howdy," but there was no one on the path from the cabin to the woods.

Thomas Lincoln and his neighbors whipsawed boards for a coffin. They buried Nancy Hanks Lincoln on a knoll not far from the cabin. There was a deer run nearby which led toward the salt lick. Today the site is a state park, and deer still use the same path—a lesson in the constant and inevitable ways of nature, a lesson young Abe Lincoln was learning as he stood at his mother's grave.

CHAPTER EIGHT

"*There Were Some Schools*"

It was only a matter of months after the death of Nancy Hanks Lincoln that Thomas attended an important meeting. The purpose of the gathering was to organize a subscription school for the children of the region. Besides Mr. Brooner, William Wood, and Thomas Lincoln, other families represented were the Turnhams, just arrived from Tennessee, the Gentrys, Lamars, Rays, Blairs, Coxes, and the Joneses, in whose store Abe had heard many heated political discussions.

Once there were sufficient children, the settlers along Little Pigeon moved quickly to provide a teacher. Andrew Crawford was hired. The school was to be held in Crawford's home, about a mile and a half from the Lincoln cabin.

A brief pause to look at Thomas Lincoln during this particular moment of his life is important, a pause which legend and many biographers seem to have denied the father when the story of the illustrious son began to unfold, but nevertheless tells much about the man. A lonely, bereft frontiersman, doubtless pondering which way to turn, hard put to make ends meet, this was not a man to scorn education, as we have been told. But rather, with the cabin womanless and chores for more hands than Tom Lincoln's could manage, he paid his share and gave his children a chance to get some "larning."

This did not in any sense make him an exception in the community. He was made the exception when the legend grew that he had no interest in education for his children.

Describing these frontiersmen in his book, *Abraham Lincoln*, Albert J. Beveridge says: "The desire that their children should get 'larning' was well-nigh a passion, second only, indeed, to their respect for law and insistence upon that regular procedure afforded by courts. . . .

"Schools were started almost as soon as churches—in fact church and school were companion influences for decency, knowledge, and morality in pioneer life."

Thomas Lincoln and his neighbors built the Pigeon Creek Baptist Church in 1819, the year they started their first school.

On a November morning in 1819 Abe and Sarah left the cabin for their first day at school in Indiana. The trees were bare except for the brown oak leaves, persistently holding on to the last. It is doubtful that "Abe and Sally" walked "hand in hand" as one biographer has so sentimentally pictured them. Nine-year-old brothers usually manage to walk several yards in front of, or behind, their sisters. Sarah probably carried the "old dog-eared speller," for the word would have gone out from the new teacher, Andrew Crawford, requesting that the children bring any books and "tracts" available from the separate cabins.

The location of the school was due west, so Abe and Sarah walked the mile and a half with the November sun warming their backs. Now and again Abe took giant steps trying to reach the shadow of his coonskin cap which always took the same step forward, leaving Abe's deerskin moccasins at the foot of the shadow just where they began.

A little more than halfway along the trail Abe and Sarah were joined by two Cox children and the Lamar boy. They had been reminded by mothers in their cabins not to say anything to the Lincolns about "their Ma's death."

Abe showed his neighbors his willow whistle and slingshot with its deerskin thongs and pouch. Each of the boys had a turn trying to shoot an acorn over the tallest oak, then they ran to catch up with the girls. Sarah and the Cox girl were wondering who else would be at school, and Sarah told about Mr. Riney's school back in Kentucky.

The mention of Mr. Riney's school caused a smile to form in Abe's eyes, and it spread across his whole face. He didn't feel peculiar and "fearsome" that the other children would laugh at him. Besides, the Coxes hadn't been to school before, and Abe had. He knew how to use the speller and "read some," and "he could write some and copy a whole book line and not make a mistake." He wanted to hear the new stories that the teacher would tell, for "all the old stories he knew by heart."

Sarah had said that Mr. Crawford's school would be like Mr. Riney's, and she was just about right. Split-log benches, high and low, provided writing desks and seats. They were arranged around the walls to allow Mr. Crawford to command an aisle which ran from the door to the fireplace.

Andrew Crawford, the teacher, tall and gentlemanly, had come to Indiana from Bardstown, so his large slate, with the alphabet in capitals and small letters, neatly written in two rows across the top, had probably come from there.

Abe's new teacher, like Mr. Riney and Caleb Hazel, had stories "aplenty" to tell from his own background. His forebears had come from Virginia. He and his cousin Josiah Crawford had been educated in the private schools in Bardstown, Kentucky. They were antislavery people and had left Kentucky for the free soil of Indiana. Andrew Crawford had been appointed a justice of the peace the summer before he began his first teaching session, so school was often "livened up" by angry neighbors who had "fallen out" and arrived "cursin' and threatenin'," demanding instant frontier justice. In such instances the scholars got a recess and doubtless much education on the laws of the wilderness, where a body's life might be endangered by a skittish hiefer that strayed into a neighbor's corn patch.

Nathaniel Grigsby, who studied Webster's old Blue-backed Speller and the first reading lessons of *The Kentucky Preceptor* with Abe at Crawford's school, went on to college, as did his older brother, Aaron, who married Sarah Lincoln. The best description of the Lincolns and the school come from his recollections.

"Sarah was brighter than Abe," Nat said, "was able to help the younger ones with their spelling and sums." Of Abe he said, "He was always early to school, had gone further with his lessons than the rest of us, and never got licked by the teacher or had to wear the dunce-cap."

All of Andrew Crawford's scholars remembered his having interlaced the lessons in "readin', writin', and cipherin'" with training in manners and better speech. He taught the formalities of introducing one person to another and how to preside at a meeting. The girls learned to curtsy and the boys learned to bow and remove their coonskin caps in the presence of ladies.

He tried, without too much success, to replace the peculiar and universally practiced frontier dialect with the refined speech passed down to him by his educated Virginia forebears. "It is not 'Whar'll I sot?' but 'Where shall I sit?'" he said. But "whar" remained "where," and "sot" was used for "sit," "set," and "sat." "The two men fought over the land boundary." They didn't "fit over'n the bounty." "Bounty means to be paid for something." When someone knocks at your cabin door, you don't say, "Whoos hyar?" You say, "Who's there?" But in this area of training Andrew Crawford was not an unqualified success. "Whoos hyar?" stuck and gave the Indianans their present nickname Hoosiers. Some of the peculiar dialect Abe would keep throughout his life, causing unsympathetic news reporters to make repeated reference to his "crude manner of speech."

Abe lost fewer of the eighty school days than most scholars. And by the light of the cabin fireplace he kept his lessons ahead "and passed us rapidly in his studies," as Nat Grigsby later recalled.

Abe's second session in Andrew Crawford's school at the age of ten found him the "strongest boy in the school for his age." During the second session, Abe graduated from the slate pencil and charcoal point to turkey and buzzard quill pens, briar-root and pokeberry ink, and paper. He began to sew together blank sheets of paper which would grow, during the next few years, to over 100 pages. He called it his sum and copy book. In it he worked arithmetic problems, copied passages from the speller, and wrote out his own thoughts. Abe tried his hand at some original verse, humorous at times, serious at others. One read: "Abraham Lincoln, his hand and pen./He will be good, but God knows

84

when." Another was: "Good boys who to their books apply/Will be great men by and by."

"While in Crawford's school," according to Nathaniel Grigsby, "he began to write, on his own account, short sentences against cruelty to animals. He was very much annoyed and pained by a habit of the boys. They would catch terrapins and put coals of fire on their backs to make them squirm. Abe chided us, told us it was wrong, and wrote a whole composition against it. He wrote that an ant's life was as sweet to it as ours to us."

But "the strongest boy in the school for his age" was no sissy. He was tall for his age. So it was quite easy for him to jump up, grab the deer antlers tied above the schoolhouse door and chin himself more times than boys two

years older, including Allen Gentry, whose father owned 1,000 acres of land, ran a store, and "shod his young'uns in store-bought shoes."

One morning before Abe arrived at school Allen Gentry decided he'd play a trick on Abe. He stood on a bench and cut almost through the leather thong that held the antlers to the log above the door. When Abe arrived Allen Gentry challenged him to a chin-up contest:

"You can go first," Abe was told as all the bystanders watched for Mr. Crawford and snickered to themselves.

Up sprang agile Abe. And with more speed landed on his back in the mud before the doorway, the antlers and thong on top of him. By the time the first side slapping and guffaws subsided Abe noticed that the thong had been cut. He rose slowly to his feet, and before Allen Gentry could take his hands out of the pockets of his store-bought breeches, Abe was wallowing him in the mud.

When somebody yelled, "Teacher in the clearin'," Abe rose, helped Gentry to his feet, and they disappeared around the corner of the schoolhouse together. The antlers were replaced by willing hands without comment from Mr. Crawford. No one seemed to notice that Abe and Allen's buckskin jackets were a "mite muddy" when they came in the schoolhouse together.

The only aftermath of the event was the nickname "Big buck of the lick" in which Abe showed evident pride, as any red-blooded frontier boy would. For everyone knew that the "big buck" was not only the strongest, but also the wisest, in a herd of deer.

The world of learning for Abe brightened significantly fourteen months after his mother's death when Sarah Bush

Johnston, his new stepmother, arrived. Thomas Lincoln had known her as a girl in Elizabethtown, Kentucky. Early in the winter of 1819 he left Dennis Hanks and William Wood to care for Abe and Sarah and returned to Elizabethtown, where on December 2 he married the widow of Daniel Johnston. She came from a better educated family than Thomas Lincoln. She was intelligent, resourceful, self-reliant, and she treated Abe and Sarah with the same kindness and love she showed her own children—Elizabeth, Matilda, and John.

Among the possessions which came to the Lincoln cabin from his new stepmother's house in Kentucky were books, five of them—*Robinson Crusoe, Pilgrim's Progress, The Arabian Nights,* Aesop's *Fables,* and the Bible. For the times and the place this was a "heap" of library to brighten the eyes of any frontier boy possessed of "soul hunger."

The dark sad memory of Nancy Hanks Lincoln, whom he always referred to as his "angel mother," lightened into sweet remembrance. Sarah Bush Lincoln "proved a good and kind mother to A," he wrote years later in his autobiography for John L. Scripps. He referred to her as his "saintly mother." The appreciation was mutual. At the age of seventy-five, looking back, she unconsciously paid great tribute to both in a summation of their relationship:

"When I landed in Indiana, the country was wild and desolate. Abe was a good boy; he didn't like physical labor, was diligent for knowledge, wished to know, and if pains and labor would get it, he was sure to get it. He was the best boy I ever saw. He read all the books he could lay his hands on. . . . I think newspapers were in Indiana as early as 1824. . . . Abe was a constant reader of them. . . . Abe . . . had no

SARAH BUSH LINCOLN

particular religion, didn't think of that question at that time, if he ever did. He never talked about it.

"He read diligently, studied in the day time, didn't after night much, went to bed early, got up early, and then read, ate his breakfast, got to work in the field with the men. . . . When he came to a passage that struck him, he would write it down on boards if he had no paper and keep it there till he did get paper, then he would rewrite it, look at it, repeat it. He had a copybook, a kind of scrap book, in which he put down all things and then preserved them. He ciphered on boards when he had no paper or no slate, and when the board would get too black, he would shave it off with a drawing knife and go on again.

"He would hear sermons, . . . come home, take the children out, get on a stump or log, and almost repeat it word for word. . . . His father made him quit sometimes, as the men quit their work. Mr. Lincoln could read a little and could scarcely write his name. . . . Abe could easily learn and long remember, and when he did learn anything he learned it well and thoroughly. . . . Abe didn't care much for crowds . . . was not very fond of girls . . . he sometimes attended church . . . he was dutiful to me always . . ."

Before the second session at Andrew Crawford's school ended " 'bout plantin' time" in the spring of 1820, Abe had read and reread Aesop's *Fables*. He recited as many as Mr. Crawford could allow time for before all the scholars. This was Abe's first practice in public speaking. It put him in a position of leadership, which he already held in being the last standing in the spelling bee, the one who could chin himself more times and who could crack bigger nuts with his teeth than any boy in school.

Years later, talking to his friend Leonard Sweet, he said, "The only book I ever read so repeatedly and with such care that I could rewrite it from memory without the loss of a single word was Aesop's *Fables*."

Andrew Crawford said good-bye to his scholars and left the Pigeon Creek settlement to find better "pickin's" and land easier to clear in the "north country on one of the forks of the Wabash River." For some parents his moving proved "a worrisome plight" because for the next two years there was no school in the settlement.

But Thomas Lincoln had a different worry—how to get Abe to put aside his books long enough to help with the

89

work of building a new and larger cabin for his enlarged family, of finishing the Pigeon Creek Baptist Church, and of growing seventeen acres of corn. Hewing logs or hoeing a row of corn, Abe's book was always nearby to read when he took a "breathin' spell."

During these years the absence of a school gave Abe time to work occasionally for his neighbors. They had something of the same problem that Thomas Lincoln had with him at home. John Romine said, "Abe worked for me, but was always reading and thinking. I used to get mad at him. Abe said to me one day that his father taught him to work but never learned him to love it."

When the crops had been gathered in the autumn of 1822, Abe, almost 14, began a session of school with a teacher named James Swaney. About all that is known of Swaney and his school is that it was four miles from the Lincoln cabin.

Abe's copybook shows that he had advanced far beyond what would be expected of a fourteen-year-old scholar. He had read and reread the books his stepmother had brought from Kentucky. He had absorbed from the Bible and Aesop's *Fables* a knowledge of the human condition, the good and the bad sides of human nature, and the necessity for understanding the ways of men in their relationship with other men. In the New Testament he had memorized the second great commandment, to treat others as he would like to be treated, and a statement which he ever after looked upon as the hope of the world: "The meek shall inherit the earth."

While he was attending James Swaney's school a relative brought from Kentucky a copy of Bailey's *Etymological*

Dictionary that had belonged to Abe's Uncle Mordecai. It must have been a most welcome and exciting legacy for the word-intoxicated Abe. It was English in origin, and its popularity had carried it through twenty-five editions. It was said to have been studied word by word by the great orator and Prime Minister William Pitt the Younger. It is not unreasonable to assume that young Abe did the same, carrying it back and forth day after day the four miles to Swaney's school.

James Swaney's school "petered out" after its one session, and Abe was left with another year to continue his self-education before his last teacher for formal schooling, Azel Dorsey, arrived at Pigeon Creek.

Azel Dorsey was an ardent abolitionist. Born in Owensboro, Kentucky, he was educated at Owensboro Seminary and later attended Transylvania University, in Lexington, Kentucky. James Gentry, Jr., older brother of Allen, whom Abe had licked at Crawford's school also attended the Owensboro Seminary. Whether his acquaintance with James Gentry was in any way responsible for his coming to the Pigeon Creek region to teach several years later is not known. Perhaps like so many antislavery Kentuckians, the free soil of Indiana, where slavery was not allowed, was incentive enough.

He first taught in Rockport, an important receiving station for runaway slaves, one of the many that dotted the free side of the Ohio River, called the Grand Trunk Line of the early underground railroad. "Ohio and the eastern part of Indiana were predestined by geography to take first place as an avenue of escape for runaway slaves," wrote

91

William Breyfogle in his *Story of the Underground Railroad.*

So high on the cliffs above Rockport, Indiana, having scouted the countryside to be sure it was free of slave hunters, young Azel Dorsey and the Reverend Wilson Craig lighted their fires to signal runaways, hiding with their canoes and rafts in slave territory, that freedom and helping hands would be waiting at the foot of the cliffs. Once on the Indiana side they were welcomed and hidden at previously selected cabins by day and helped northward toward Canada, safe from slave hunters, by night. Thus Abe's last teacher and the Reverend Wilson Craig along with Levi Coffin, James Birney, John Fairchild, the Reverend John Rankin, and others in the same region kept the Grand Trunk Line to freedom, across the Ohio River, open for those who risked all and endured all to find freedom.

In the autumn of 1825 Azel Dorsey moved to Gentryville and prepared the old Crawford school for opening after "gatherin'-in time." It was also a convenient location for underground activity. From Rockport, 15 miles away, a fugitive, having crossed the river, could easily arrive at the first inland layover station the same night. These few miles inland made capture much less likely. Slave hunters, dealing in human beings for reward or resale, were prone to make their living with as little work as possible. They preferred the easier hunting near points of entrance.

The influence that Azel Dorsey had upon sixteen-year-old Abe, and indirectly the future of the history of the United States, is impossible to estimate. "What's them two find to talk about so long, sottin' atop the fence hour after hour?" Thomas Lincoln asked Sarah as twilight settled

over Abe and Azel Dorsey across the corn lot from the Lincoln cabin.

"Abe is questionin' and listenin' and then listenin' and questionin'," Sarah replied as she took the wooden milk pail from him and prepared to strain the milk.

"But if Mr. Jefferson said he had 'sworn on the altar of God eternal hostility against every form of tyranny over the mind of man,' like my history book says, why didn't he do more about slavery?" Abe asked in the gathering darkness.

"He tried hard," Azel Dorsey replied. "He wanted to get it abolished in Virginia, but he only got a law forbidding importing more slaves into the state. And it didn't last long or amount to much. He was in France when the Constitution was written, so he didn't have any say there. But when he was President in 1808, the date when the Constitution said no more slaves would be imported, he tried hard to enforce that law."

The men and issues of the day, thoughtful reflections upon what the founders of the country had intended, how far it had come, what directions it was taking, where it would go—these were the topics being talked about before hundreds of frontier firesides, at country stores, at crossroads where natives quizzed travelers, and on a rail fence

93

across the corn lot from Tom Lincoln's cabin where Abe and Azel Dorsey talked till dark.

There were letters and speeches of Washington, Franklin, Jefferson, Daniel Webster, and Henry Clay in the paper from Lexington, Kentucky, and even in Abe's schoolbook *The Kentucky Preceptor*. Abe had scratched them on his mind "like on steel," not to be erased. Azel Dorsey marveled at the boy. With pride and feeling Abe would quote one of his heroes, then ask, "But why didn't he do more?"

It was in Dorsey's school that Abe first heard and discussed some of *The Revised Statutes of Indiana*, two years before he borrowed a copy from David Turnham to devour mentally its 500 pages.

It was the first lawbook Abe ever saw. It began with the Declaration of Independence, the Constitution, the Ordinance of 1787, which had made Indiana forever free territory:

"There shall be neither slavery nor involuntary servitude in the said territory, otherwise than in the punishment of crimes, whereof the party shall have been duly convicted: provided always, that any person escaping into the same, from whom labor or service is lawfully claimed in any one of the original States, such fugitive may be lawfully reclaimed and conveyed to the person claiming his or her labor of service, as aforesaid."

Abe was the "oldest and biggest and best" scholar in Azel Dorsey's school. And long afterward when Dorsey left Indiana and taught in Schuyler County, Illinois, he talked about his "prize scholar."

The boy who had lectured to his friends that "an ant's

94

life was as precious to it as theirs was to them" took to Mr. Dorsey. Mr. Dorsey reminded him of Caleb Hazel. What he said had to do with people and how they were treated or mistreated.

He said that Indiana wasn't free. "Look at the census taken five years ago," he said. "There were a hundred and ninety slaves in Spencer County alone, and there are probably still that many." Abe listened as Azel Dorsey continued: "This statement that the territory would be forever free was made by the Congress for all the states that would develop in the territory. But the Indiana legislature has laws of its own."

Mr. Dorsey flipped the pages and read several laws: "'A Negro youth may be indentured as a servant until he comes of age.' Indentured is just a fancy word for limited slavery, seven years or ten years or half of one's life. That's why Negro families stick close together while passing through the territory. If they get separated, the children might be enslaved. Here's a law which says Negroes can't vote, can't serve on juries, cannot testify in court against a white man."

Azel Dorsey slammed the statutes of Indiana down on the puncheon bench that served as his desk. "And over in Illinois, at Shawneetown, slave labor to work the salt mines is legal. That's why when escaped slaves cross the Ohio, half-starved and sometimes half-dead from fatigue or injury, they want to keep going north, north to the lakes, and across the lakes to Canada and real freedom."

Sixteen-year-old Abe would remember Azel Dorsey's feelings. They were his feelings, too. One day, yet far in the future, he would put these long and troublesome feel-

95

ings in Mr. Riney's short words for all men to understand: "I would not be a slave, therefore I would not be a master."

Mr. Dorsey spoke slowly when he began. He warmed to his subject, his eyes brightened, and his voice seemed to come directly from his heart. Abe began to imitate his style when he entertained his friends.

Mr. Dorsey introduced Abe to Scott's *Lessons in Elocution*. Here Abe found instruction for effective public speaking. The opening chapters emphasized the necessity for the speaker's presenting a "precise idea" with clarity and simplicity. It recommended "modification of gesture" so as to not detract from the content, and "distinction of enunciation, right emphasis, pausing between sentences." Sample pieces for practice included Cicero, Demosthenes, and a

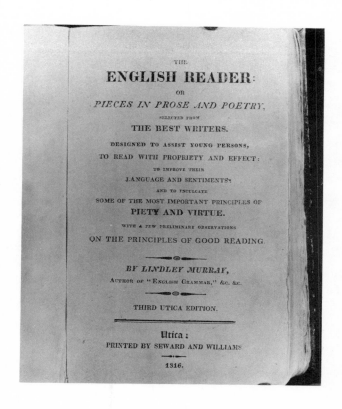

THE

ENGLISH READER:

OR

PIECES IN PROSE AND POETRY,

SELECTED FROM

THE BEST WRITERS.

DESIGNED TO ASSIST YOUNG PERSONS,

TO READ WITH PROPRIETY AND EFFECT:

TO IMPROVE THEIR

LANGUAGE AND SENTIMENTS:

AND TO INCULCATE

SOME OF THE MOST IMPORTANT PRINCIPLES OF

PIETY AND VIRTUE.

WITH A FEW PRELIMINARY OBSERVATIONS

ON THE PRINCIPLES OF GOOD READING.

BY LINDLEY MURRAY,

AUTHOR OF "ENGLISH GRAMMAR," &c. &c.

THIRD UTICA EDITION.

Utica:

PRINTED BY SEWARD AND WILLIAMS

1816.

number of orations from Shakespeare's plays. It was here in Dorsey's school that the peculiar blend of Abe's humility and strength of conviction molded the style which would in later years command the ears of men and the world.

It was in Dorsey's school also that Abe first saw Murray's *English Grammar* and the same author's *English Reader*, which he referred back upon in his adult life as "the best schoolbook ever put into the hands of an American boy."

Outside the school Azel Dorsey was involved in activity which Abe could scarcely have let pass without participation. How many nights did Abe accompany Dorsey along the road to Rockport, listen for an owl's hoot in a given series of threes or a whistle from the edge of the clearing, near a predesignated cabin, and hurry one or more fugitives, dripping wet from the mighty Ohio's spray and half-starved, to a cabin to be warmed and fed?

Of the conductors of the early underground railroad over the Grand Trunk Line into Indiana and Ohio, William Breyfogle says: ". . . as with people everywhere and at all times, there was an element of mischief and frivolity in them, not wholly satisfied by neighborhood roof-raisings and camp meetings. Life on a frontier is always hard, often dangerous. But worse than either of these, it is monotonous." They had to contend "not only with physical monotony," he writes, "but with an exacting moral and religious code that set its face . . . against virtually any kind of excitement or fun. The one exception made was in favor of helping fugitive slaves to freedom.

"Certainly, the conductors of the Underground Railroad acted on principle. But if they were honest with themselves, they must privately have admitted that they hugely enjoyed the work, as well. With a good conscience, a nonviolent Quaker could bear arms, and a law-abiding Presbyterian could help despoil his neighbor of what was legal property."

Aside from the lessons of Caleb Hazel and Azel Dorsey which Abe had taken to heart, would he, proud of his physical prowess in wrestling, log rolling and barn raising, have missed the excitement of his companion-teacher's activity? That he never talked about it, that he did not include it in his brief effacing statements of his early life—these do not provide the answer. It was a part of his environment and world. It was part of the activity of settlers who had come to Spencer County, Indiana, because they hated slavery. He was one of them, more than the exception.

Thomas Lincoln complained to Sarah, "Abe spends so much time sottin' on the rail fence talkin' to Azel Dorsey, he ain't dug no sassafras root to bile for spring tonic."

So Thomas Lincoln had no regrets when Azel Dorsey moved across the Wabash to Shawneetown, near the mouth of the Saline River. Azel Dorsey had heard that the slaves in the salt mines were penned at night in the dark damp caverns, that once inside, they never saw the light of day again. He wondered if there was anything that could ever be done about it. He left Abe his copy of Scott's *Lesson in Elocution* and Lindley Murray's *Grammar* and *English Reader*. When he asked Abe about his future plans, Abe said, "I think I'll help Pa with the crops and then go work on the river." Meaning, of course, the Ohio.

"Always remember," Azel Dorsey told Abe when they said good-bye, "that lack of a school needn't hamper your learning."

CHAPTER NINE

"*I Did Not Know Much*"

Lincoln began his river experience as a ferryman at the mouth of Anderson's Creek, at the little town of Troy. His wage was $6 a month. As teachers then averaged $8 a month, this wage was quite respectable for the time. It was more than could be earned by regular day labor, and the job offered Abe adventure and the chance to see new places.

Who can doubt that ferryman Lincoln watched for lights to flare and made many a trip to the Kentucky shore under cover of darkness, ferrying hunted human cargo without charge? In the gentle curve of the great Ohio between Grandview and the mouth of Anderson's Creek, at Troy, where Abe tied up his ferry, there sometimes floated into the backwater stark evidence of the meaning of screams in the night, the bark of slave hunters' rifles, or an empty row-boat or raft floating past—flotsam which only yesterday had been living dreams of freedom.

How long Lincoln remained in the employment of James Taylor, owner of the Anderson's Creek ferry is not known.

The "quarter section-two dollar an acre" law for the land of the Northwest Territory that had prompted Thomas

Lincoln to move from Kentucky to Indiana also stirred others. It started "the great migration" which brought 3,000 flatboats a year down the Ohio during the 1820's. The whole of "America seems to be breaking up and moving westward," wrote Morris Birkbeck, in *Notes on a Journey in America.* "We are seldom out of sight, as we travel on this grand track towards the Ohio, of family groups, behind and before us."

It is certain that by the spring of 1827 Lincoln had built a flatboat and was in business for himself. This certainty is not based upon the oft-repeated story by many biographers of how Lincoln made a dollar "in a single day" by taking two strangers and their trunks to the middle of the Ohio to board a passing steamboat. The fact that he was in business for himself and not an employee of Taylor is a matter of court record. For, in the spring of 1827, Abraham Lincoln was named defendant in the case of *Kentucky v. Lincoln,* and charged with operating a ferry without a license.

John T. Dill was licensed to operate a ferry in Kentucky waters, and Kentucky claimed the whole width of the Ohio to the low-water mark on the Indiana shore. When Lincoln appeared before Squire Samuel Pate in the log-cabin court on the Kentucky shore, he was acquitted on the grounds that he had only carried passengers to the middle of the river to board steamboats and therefore had not violated the law which stated that a license was required to "carry persons over the river."

In 1828, aged nineteen, Abe Lincoln was a graduate of the river school. He was hired by James Gentry, one of the wealthiest and most enterprising settlers in Spencer County,

to handle the bow oar of a produce-laden flatboat bound for New Orleans. Lincoln was paid $8 per month and expenses for the three months' trip. The position of bow oarsman made Lincoln the responsible person, equivalent to captain. This was no job that a man as businesslike and enterprising as James Gentry would entrust to a backcountry inexperienced rail splitter. It required more than physical strength. Knowledge of currents, ability to deal with crafty traders in New Orleans, an understanding of human nature sufficient to avoid traps of promoters, con men, and thieves were all prerequisites of a successful voyage and return.

Yet legend has been successful in keeping Lincoln cutting away at the forest's edge, splitting rails, kept in virtual paternal slavery until statute freed him at twenty-one. The reason for this becomes plain when the sudden popularity of the "rail-splitter candidate" is examined. It spread like a prairie fire from the moment John Hanks showed up at the Illinois State Convention on May 10, 1860, displaying two fence rails, trailing a banner which proclaimed that they had been split by "Abraham Lincoln, the rail-candidate, whose father was the first pioneer in Macon County, Illinois." After an Ohio delegate at the National Republican Convention in Chicago, later that same month, nominated Lincoln for President as "a man who can split rails and maul Democrats" it was too late to bring out a ferryboat pole or a flatboat bow oar.

Besides, there were many more voters who had split rails than had handled a bow oar. But still another reason deserves consideration. Between the years of Lincoln's experience as a riverman (1827–30), and 1860, when he submitted his brief autobiographical sketches, the flatboatman and the keelboatman had lost much of their stature. Their character had begun to lose its indispensable and daring quality as early as 1811. It was in this year that Captain Nicholas Roosevelt took the steamboat *New Orleans* from Pittsburgh down the Ohio and Mississippi to New Orleans. As use of the paddle-wheeler grew, rivermen became choppers and stokers, feeding the fireboxes under the boilers that powered the steamboats. Some became "shore drifters" and tramps, preying on or pilfering river goods. Mike Fink had lost his heroic quality and died a drunken murderer at the hands of a gunsmith named Talbott. It is therefore easy to understand why Lincoln saw little point in emphasizing that part of his life in Indiana which went beyond swinging an ax and enduring "pretty pinchy times." Many voters in 1860 were too young to remember the "heroic riverman"; they knew him only as a "river rat" and a renegade.

In a one-page autobiography written in December, 1859, Abe wrote: "Of course when I came of age I did not know much." He concluded the paragraph on his education by saying that what advance he had made was "picked up from time to time under pressure of necessity."

From the autumn of 1826 until Abe "came of age" in 1830, the time was spent doing a great deal of picking up. For all who knew him remembered of these years, both at home and as a ferryman and river man on the Ohio, that "he read everything he could get his hands on," borrowing

STEAM BOAT ON THE MISSISSIPPI.

books from neighbors in such quantity as to necessitate "tieing them up in his bandana and carrying them home swung over his shoulder at the end of a pole."

Besides the books already mentioned as having been used in school and out, there was a sufficient supply available among his friends and acquaintances to satisfy his needs, and surely within a much shorter radius than "fifty miles."

"Many of the local pioneer families," writes one educator and historian of Lincoln's Indiana, "took great pride in sending at least one child out of the state to school; and their textbooks were brought home and passed around." Among Abe's contemporaries who attended schools of higher learning were the Grigsbys, one or more of the Gentrys, and the Ray sisters, including Abe's close friend, Elizabeth. There were also men like James Blair, who had been educated in the East before they moved West. In an environment where companionship and social contact were at such premium that people would walk miles to "set awhile" and visit, Abe's arrival to borrow a book or his returning it and spending time in talking over its contents was without doubt a most welcome event.

From David Turnham he borrowed *Arabian Nights*, which he read aloud to his stepmother. Josiah Crawford, educated in the Academy at Bardstown, Kentucky, had an interesting selection of books. It was from Crawford that Abe borrowed Ramsey's *Life of Washington*. The book was damaged by rain, and Abe paid for it by stripping corn for two days. William Jones, who was a partner in Gentry's store, had studied at Vincennes University. He supplied Abe with the newspapers from Lexington, Kentucky. He

104

also gave Abe a copy of Grimshaw's *History of the United States.*

Books of the time were all designed and advertised for use by scholars and general readers—for school and home use. Most of the authors seemed to be compelled to do the whole job; they compiled their books as though each would be the only one their scholar or reader would ever see. This was particularly true of those books which dealt with reading and writing.

The nature, intention, and completeness of the content of every book, whether speller or *Introduction to Astronomy*, were directed toward teaching four great lessons in addition to its subject matter: First, God or some guiding Providence cared for creation and was working out His or Its grand design in history. In this design there was a higher law for the guidance of human beings which they should seek to understand. Secondly, man had been created just "a little below the angels." He was gifted with power to reason and conscience to direct that reason. If he used the powers given him, there were scarcely any heights beyond his reach in making a better world. Thirdly, failure to use these powers to the utmost, not only for the betterment of oneself, but for the whole of mankind, was a sin against the Creator and a flouting of His purposes.

The fourth lesson—and to an ambitious boy, growing up in the wilderness of Indiana, perhaps the most impressive— was that God had chosen this land, America, for the unique and precious experiment—democracy for a whole big country to demonstrate to the world that it could work. The American people had been chosen—as the Creator had once before chosen a people to carry out His will. And it was important beyond all else. "The last, best hope of earth" were the words Lincoln would use one day when the lesson seemed as though it might have been taught in vain.

These were the lessons of any one of dozens of history and literature books available to Abe. He is known to have studied William Grimshaw's *History of the United States*. This was only one of fifteen one-volume histories of the United States circulating at the time. Grimshaw's itself ran through sixteen editions. It included astronomy, geography, exploration, the growth of the colonies—lashing out violently against the colonists for the introduction of slavery. It told the marvelous story of the American Revolution, described as the War of Independence. It included a study of America's "own" literature, science, and art. It closed with the admonition: "Let us not only declare by words, but demonstrate by our actions, that 'All men are created equal; that they are endowed by their Creator, with the same inalienable rights: that among these are life, liberty, and the pursuit of happiness.'"

For advanced reading there were more than thirty patriotic anthologies printed during the decades following the Revolution. Abe had known *The Kentucky Preceptor* from the days of Mr. Riney's school. It was one of the books he himself owned, along with *The Columbian Class Book,* Murray's *Grammer*, Kirkman's *Grammar*, and Murray's *English Reader. The Columbian Orator* from which a slave boy named Frederick Douglass, born in Tuckahoe, Maryland, in 1818, had taught himself to read, was also available.

As one reviews the contents of *The Columbian Class*

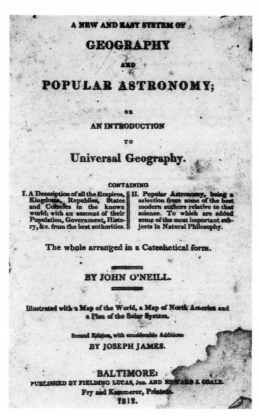

A NEW AND EASY SYSTEM OF

GEOGRAPHY

AND

POPULAR ASTRONOMY;

OR

AN INTRODUCTION

TO

Universal Geography.

CONTAINING

I. A Description of all the Empires, Kingdoms, Republics, States and Colonies in the known world; with an account of their Population, Government, History, &c. from the best authorities.

II. Popular Astronomy, being a selection from some of the best modern authors relative to that science. To which are added some of the most important subjects in Natural Philosophy.

The whole arranged in a Catechetical form.

BY JOHN O'NEILL.

Illustrated with a Map of the World, a Map of North America and a Plan of the Solar System.

Second Edition, with considerable Additions

BY JOSEPH JAMES.

BALTIMORE:

PUBLISHED BY FIELDING LUCAS, Jun. AND EDWARD J. COALE.

Fry and Kammerer, Printers.

1812.

Book and Murray's *English Reader*, there comes the feeling that either book provided a liberal education. Bound in buckskin, the first containing 355 pages, the latter 366, the pages filled with small print, each book contains more than eighty selections of geographical, historical, scientific, and biographical extracts, ranging from writings of Pliny the Elder and Cicero down to Jefferson, Webster and Henry Clay. Poetry of Pope, Young, Shakespeare, and Tennyson is plentiful in both.

The topics range from a scientific explanation of Lake

Asphaltites (Dead Sea) to a speech of the great Indian Chief Logan before Governor Dunsmore, beginning with the sentence: "My cabin, since I first had one of my own, has ever been open to any white man who wanted shelter."

Abe's favorite, Murray's *English Reader*, carries the following message on the title page:

"Designed to assist young readers to read with propriety and effect; to improve their language and sentiments; and to inculcate some of the most important principles of piety and virtue." After an introduction on proper methods of reading—degrees of slowness, pauses, emphasis, tones, and the manner of reading verse—it begins with a selection of sentences for practice, the first of which is: "The acquisition of knowledge is one of the most honourable occupations of youth."

Besides the schoolbooks available during his last years in Indiana, he borrowed *The Revised Statutes of Indiana* which Azel Dorsey had first introduced him to. His appreciation of law took him to the libraries of two Eastern-educated lawyers, Judges John Pitcher and John A. Brackenridge.

According to John Pitcher's family, he was attracted to Lincoln, "advised him regarding his studies, and made his four hundred volume library available to young Abe." Pitcher lived at Rockport, easily accessible to Abe during his years on the Ohio and not by any means impossible from Pigeon Creek.

Attorney and later Judge John Pitcher had migrated to Indiana from Connecticut. He was college-educated and had studied law in the offices of the great judge, teacher, and compiler of lawbooks Tapping Reeve, in Litchfield,

Connecticut, where John C. Calhoun and Aaron Burr had also studied. John Pitcher "was the ablest man who lived in Spencer County in Lincoln's day, and had the best education possible for a man of his time." It was to Pitcher that Abe showed his essay entitled "American Government." After reading it, Pitcher is credited with saying, "The world couldn't beat it." At the age of ninety-three, when his would-be apprentice had become America's most famous man, Judge Pitcher recalled that Abe had once expressed a desire to study law in his office, but had not because of "his poverty at the time."

John A. Brackenridge lived in Boonville, 12 miles from the Lincoln cabin. Brackenridge was educated at Princeton. His law library of 457 volumes was available to Abe.

On February 12, 1830, Abe celebrated his twenty-first birthday. Thomas Lincoln, who had been subject to recurring fever and ague in the damp lowlands of Indiana, was planning to move to Illinois. (The indolence of Thomas Lincoln's later years may well have been the result of lingering malaria.) On his twenty-first birthday, William Wood, who had always been a keen observer of his young neighbor and friend, said to Abe, "Now you are a man, but when you were a boy, you were a man, too."

Lincoln would continue his education among new friends on the Illinois prairie which the early Jesuit missionaries had called "a sea of grass and flowers." "Only the poet," wrote Francis Grierson, "could feel the charm of her . . . only a far-seeing statesman could predict her future greatness. . . . Across its bosom came the covered wagons with their human freight, arriving and departing like ships between the shores of strange, mysterious worlds."

109

CHAPTER TEN

"Thought He Could Not Succeed"

In March, 1830, Abe left Indiana driving one of the three ox-drawn wagons that made up the caravan of Thomas Lincoln and the Hall family 200 miles to Macon County, Illinois. There on a bluff above the Sangamon River, a few miles west of Decatur, a new cabin was built.

The location of the new settlement was where the dark timberland gave way to the vast prairie, extending its mystery, omens, and promise as far as the eye could see.

Around the new cabin fifteen acres of the rich prairie loam responded to plow and spade. But before crops were gathered in autumn, Thomas Lincoln, who had left Indiana to escape the damp land that bred ague and fever, was "mighty poorly." The frontier which made some men strong weakened others and broke them. After one terrible winter in Macon County, during which the cattle, deer, and wild turkey froze to death and "only the wolves survived," Thomas Lincoln moved to Coles County.

Abe had spent some of his first year in Illinois as friend and employee of William Warnick, the sheriff of Macon County. He studied *The Revised Code of Laws of Illinois,*

and during this year he spoke in an impromptu political debate with a man named Posy in the town of Decatur. The topic was the advantage to be gained by river dredging to improve transportation. The long, gangly countryman's delivery held his audience. They understood his reasoning, couched in simple language and story that was a part of them.

The successful riverman from the Ohio did not long remain unknown in his new surroundings. In the spring of 1831, Abe, along with John Hanks and John D. Johnston, were hired by Dennis Offut to build a flatboat, 80 by 18 feet, and float it down the Sangamon River to Beardstown, on the Illinois. There it was loaded with produce, and Abe made his second trip to New Orleans. On the Mississippi journey Dennis Offut discovered that Abe's mental powers equaled his physical strength. Offut persuaded Abe to join him in a mercantile and milling project at New Salem—a town on the Sangamon.

New Salem was a town of about twenty families. Both its founders, James Rutledge, the grandson of the first Chief Justice of the Supreme Court, and the Reverend John Cameron, were Southerners, as was most of the population. The hope of New Salem rested upon the navigability of the Sangamon, a project into which Abe Lincoln threw himself wholly—piloting the cabin steamer *Talisman* to a landing place near Springfield, then downstream to Beardstown. He also made the dredging of the river a platform in his first campaign speech.

Abraham Lincoln lived in New Salem for about six years. During this time he was merchant, surveyor, postmaster, captain of a company in the Black Hawk War, and legislator. Beginning the practice of drawing deeds and bonds soon after his arrival in New Salem, he continued this practice and mastered the study of law, using the law library of John T. Stuart. Years later people living between New Salem and Springfield recalled that going to and fro with books borrowed from Stuart, Abe sat astride his rawboned bay horse, reading aloud as he went.

He joined the New Salem Debating Society and won debates and admiration from his elders and contemporaries, five of whom attended the state college at Jacksonville, Illinois. Robert Rutledge, one of those attending the college, who agreed with Denton Offut "that Lincoln knew more than any man he had ever seen," left a description of his style of speaking: "As he rose to speak, his tall form towered above the little assembly. Both hands were thrust down deep into the pockets of his pantaloons. A perceptible smile at once lit up the faces of the audience, for all anticipated the relation of some humorous story, but he opened

112

up the discussion in splendid style, to the infinite astonish-
ment of his friends. As he warmed to his subject, his hands
would forsake his pockets, and would enforce his ideas by
awkward gestures; but would very soon seek their resting
place. He pursued the question with reason and argument
so pithy and forcible that all were amazed."

James Rutledge, the president of the debating society,
confided to his wife after he had heard Abe speak that there
was "more than wit and fun in Abe's head, that he was
already a fine speaker."

JOHN T. STUART

Mentor Graham, the village schoolmaster, nine years Abe's senior, a lover of learning, was impressed. He and Abe became close friends. Legend later gave Graham credit for having an important part in Lincoln's quick mastery of the higher mathematics necessary for surveying and his mastery of English language and grammar. Lincoln's copybook provides evidence that his understanding of mathematics was beyond Graham's before he arrived in Illinois. And nothing Graham or anyone else in New Salem left in writing even approaches the simple and distinctive style of Lincoln's first address to the voters of Sangamon County. One suspects that a mutual love of learning drew Abe and Mentor Graham together.

When Lincoln had been in New Salem just over six months, his friends encouraged him to become a candidate for the legislature. He announced his candidacy on March 9, 1832 in the Sangamon *Journal*:

Upon the subject of education, not presuming to dictate any plan or system respecting it, I can only say that I view it as the most important subject, which we as a people can be engaged in. That every man may receive at least, a modern education, and thereby be enabled to read the histories of his own and other countries, by which he may duly appreciate the value of our free institutions, appears to be an object of vital importance, even on this account alone, to say nothing of the advantages and satisfaction to be derived from all being able to read the scriptures and other works, both of a religious and moral nature, for themselves. For my part, I desire to see the time when education,

114

and by its means, morality, sobriety, enterprise and industry, shall become much more general than at present, and should be gratified to have it in my power to contribute something to the advancement of any measure which might have a tendency to accelerate the happy period. . . .

Every man is said to have his peculiar ambition. Whether it be true or not, I can say for one that I have no other so great as that of being truly esteemed of my fellow men, by rendering myself worthy of their esteem. How far I shall succeed in gratifying this ambition, is yet to be developed. I am young and unknown to many of you. I was born and have ever remained in the most humble walks of life. I have no wealthy or popular relations to recommend me. My case is thrown exclusively upon the independent voters of this county, and if elected they will have conferred a favor upon me, for which I shall be unremitting in my labors to compensate. But if the good people in their wisdom shall see fit to keep me in the background, I have been too familiar with disappointments to be very much chagrined. Your friend and fellow-citizen,
New Salem, March 9, 1832.

A. LINCOLN.

He concluded the message in a manner which was to be typical of Lincoln throughout his life—coming always to allow final judgment to rest with "the good people in their wisdom."

Here already was the stamp of common sense, simplicity,

and keen analytical reasoning, voiced with a humility which always appeared to leave his audience the final decision. The men who were his secretaries when he was President, John G. Nicolay and John Hay, said of his March 9 announcement: "This is almost precisely the style of his later years . . . his language was at twenty-two, as it was thirty years later, the simple and manly attire of his thought, with little attempt at ornament and none at disguise."

Abraham Lincoln had lived a little more than two-fifths of his life when he ran for his first political office and was defeated. The vast endless prairie horizon of Illinois gave him that moment of bewilderment and feeling of smallness which it was likely to carry to men on its wind message, heard in the night or seen in the day bending the long bearded grass as though to break it. Would the prairie break him too? He wondered if he "would succeed."

Almost three-fifths of his life remained, thirty-three years to keep on doing "the very best I know how—the very best I can; and I mean to keep doing so until the end. If the end brings me out all right what is said against me won't amount to anything. If the end brings me out wrong ten angels swearing I was right would make no difference."

During all these years his education continued. When Sangamon County needed a surveyor to lay out new roads and towns, Abe accepted the job and, as he described it, "procured a compass and chain, studied Flint, and Gibson a little, and went at it." Flint and Gibson were the two standard textbooks of the day on surveying.

During his three years as surveyor, he was going "at it" in other fields. Defeated for the state legislature in 1832, he was elected two years later in 1834. It was also in 1834 that he began to read law seriously. In 1836 he was licensed to practice law. He was elected to three more terms in the state legislature. When the legislature was not in session, he was making a name for himself as a lawyer. In 1846 he was elected to the United States Congress. In Congress he spoke out against the Mexican War: "This is no war of defense, but one of unnecessary and offensive aggression." He considered it, as did his idol, Henry Clay, being carried out "for the purpose of propagating slavery." Perhaps his other most significant act in Congress was to introduce a bill to free slaves in the District of Columbia. Support for the bill never developed and nothing came of it. He did not stand for reelection. He had learned much of the workings of politics, but for now he was happy to return to Illinois and use his skill to become one of the state's best lawyers. The Republican Party nominated Abe Lincoln to run for the Senate. The question that had split the South Fork Baptist Church had now split the nation. Gathering storm clouds of dissension shadowed the land. The people who would elect Mr. Lincoln or his opponent, Stephen A. Douglas, were divided on the question of slavery. The person who would win the election must offer something to both sides. When Abe's friends read his acceptance speech, they begged him not to make it. It would satisfy neither group and lose the election for him. "And the objective of an election was to win," they said.

On June 16, 1858, he delivered the speech as he had written it. Its theme was built upon the statement "A house divided against itself cannot stand. I believe this government cannot endure permanently half slave and half free." His friends were right. He did not win the election to the

Senate. But the unshakable fortress of conviction stood firm. That unswerving sense of right that young Abe had seen in Caleb Hazel the people began to see in Abe.

CHAPTER ELEVEN

President Lincoln

When America was approaching the great crisis of an impending civil war in 1859, men who heard preachers in pulpits and at camp meetings issue their prophecies that "the Lord will raise up another Moses" began to look for the man who destiny would raise up to lead in time of that crisis. In 1859, Jess W. Fell, a university-educated lawyer, who had once been a teacher himself, was the first to put forward the name of Abraham Lincoln as the man for the Presidency in this difficult period.

Fell, the first lawyer to settle in Menard County, Illinois, first knew Lincoln as a fellow state legislator at Vandalia. He had come to respect Lincoln's keen intelligence and profound wisdom. Yet when Fell finally extracted from Lincoln a one-page autobiography for release to Eastern papers, in December, 1859, it was accompanied by a note which began: "Herewith is a little sketch, as you requested. There is not much of it, for the reason, I suppose, that there is not much of me."

Little more than a year later, on February 11, 1861, Abraham Lincoln stood on the train platform in Springfield and said farewell to Illinois and his friends. He was going to

I was born Feb. 12, 1809, in Hardin county, Kentucky. My parents were both born in Virginia, of undistinguished families—second families, perhaps I should say. My mother, who died in my tenth year, was of a family of the name of Hanks, some of whom now reside in Adams, and others in Macon counties, Illinois— My paternal grandfather, Abraham Lincoln, emigrated from Rockingham county, Virginia, to Kentucky, about 1781 or 2, where, a year or two later, he was killed by indians, not in battle, but by stealth, when he was laboring to open a farm in the forest— His ancestors, who were quakers, went to Virginia from Berks county, Pennsylvania— An effort to identify them with the New England family of the same name ended in nothing more definite, than a similarity of Christian names in both families, such as Enoch, Levi, Mordecai, Solomon, Abraham, and the like—

My father, at the death of his father, was but six years of age; and he grew up, literally without education— He removed from Kentucky to what is now Spencer county, Indiana, in my eighth year— We reached our new home about the time the State came into the union— It was a wild region, with many bears and other wild animals, still in the woods— There I grew up. There were some schools, so called; but no qualification was ever required of a teacher beyond "readin, writin, and cipherin" to the Rule of Three— If a straggler supposed to understand latin, happened to sojourn in

Washington to be inaugurated as the sixteenth President of the United States. Earlier he had said in a parable regarding the Union of states: "'A house divided against itself cannot stand.' I believe this government cannot endure permanently half slave and half free. I do not expect the Union to be dissolved—I do not expect the house to fall." Now the house was dividing; the states were separating, North and South.

From the platform he waved farewell. "I now leave, not knowing when or whether ever I may return, with a task before me greater than that which rested upon Washington. Without the assistance of that Divine Being who ever attended him, I cannot succeed. With that assistance, I cannot fail."

So long ago the boy had hurried to Gentry's store on Little Pigeon Creek in the wilderness of Indiana to read what Henry Clay was saying and doing in Washington. Now the message of "my beau ideal of a statesman," as Lincoln called this second of his heroes, would be repeated again and yet again by Lincoln: "This Union is to last, I trust, forever."

In one of his schoolbooks, *The Columbian Orator,* young Abe had found and remembered a quotation from Thomas Jefferson, speaking on the subject of slavery: "I tremble for my country when I remember that God is just." Now the man faced the task of saving "the principles of Jefferson from total overthrow in this nation."

The winds of war and controversy had blown against his heroes but had not overwhelmed them. On that bleak February day, in 1861, Lincoln's neighbors crowded in to say good-bye. The sunshine and the storm of quiet wilderness and singing prairie had seasoned him in body, mind, and soul. He was ready for the task before him. The winds of war and controversy would not overwhelm him. He would use the ability to listen, learned in the wilderness and from Mr. Riney, to hear a plaintive cry for help in what other men heard as grumblings to be quieted. He would hear the crashing of a flood tide of tears upon the heart of a people divided by a great civil war; he would hear the cry of the wounded, the weeping of the mother for her son, above the rumble of men marching, above the thunder of cannon fire.

Now he was the leader of men; he had listened to their feelings, what they felt but could not put into words. Now the leader must interpret men to themselves. What he had received from them as mist he must give back as rain. Homely stories he had heard at country stores, barn raisings, and hog butcherings, he would now retell to bring smiles to the faces of grim, haggard men. The lessons he had learned he would polish into deathless rhythms to teach "that this nation, under God, shall have a new birth of freedom— and that government of the people, by the people, for the people, shall not perish from the earth."

He knew the price of peace, but nothing in his language cried for "the spoils of war." While others pronounced their curses, hates, and tirades for revenge, he coaxed beauty from the very fruits of war: "With malice toward none; with charity for all; with firmness in the right, as God gives us to see the right, let us strive to finish the work we are in; to bind up the nation's wounds; to care for him who shall have borne the battle, and for his widow, and his orphan—to do all which may achieve and cherish a just and lasting peace, among ourselves, and with all nations."

Abraham Lincoln had educated himself for his moment of greatness. Today he is a teacher—teaching the world the miracle of the great man, the potential for greatness, and what vast goodness and strength can be contained in one human heart.

Bibliography

There have been more than 4,000 books written about Abraham Lincoln. No other American even approaches that number, and in the world's literature only Jesus of Nazareth, Alexander the Great, and Napoleon Bonaparte have been the subject of more books. It is therefore very difficult to attempt anything except a narrow and selective list of books for a bibliography. The bibliography which follows is recommended for the beginner rather than the informed or addicted Lincoln scholar.

For His Early Years:
  Daugherty, James, *Abraham Lincoln.* New York, Viking Press, 1943.
  Sandburg, Carl, *Abe Lincoln Grows Up.* New York, Harcourt Brace Jovanovich, Inc., 1931.
For His Middle Years:
  Duff, John J. A., *A. Lincoln, Prairie Lawyer.* New York, Holt, Rinehart & Winston, 1960.

Sandburg, Carl, *Abraham Lincoln: The Prairie Years.* New York, Harcourt Brace Jovanovich, Inc., 1926.

Simon, Paul, *Lincoln's Preparation for Greatness: The Illinois Legislative Years.* Urbana, University of Illinois Press, 1965.

For His Years of Greatness:

Randall, J. G., *Lincoln, The President: Springfield to Gettysburg.* Glouster, Peter Smith, 1945. 2 vols.

Sandburg, Carl, *Abraham Lincoln: The War Years.* New York, Harcourt Brace Jovanovich, 1939. 2 vols.

For His Tragic Death:

Bishop, Jim, *The Day Lincoln Was Shot.* New York, Harper & Row Publishers, Inc., 1955.

Eisenshiml, Otto, *Why Was Lincoln Murdered?* New York, Grosset & Dunlap, Inc., 1957.

One Volume Biographies:

Charnwood, Lord, *Abraham Lincoln.* R. West, 1973.

Thomas, Benjamin P., *Abraham Lincoln.* New York, Alfred A. Knopf, Inc., 1952.

Lincoln's Speeches and Letters:

Angle, Paul M., and Miers, Earl S., eds., *The Living Lincoln.* New Brunswick, Rutgers University Press, 1955.

Basler, Roy P., ed., *Collected Works of Abraham Lincoln.* New Brunswick, Rutgers University Press, 1953, 9 vols.

Associated Interest:

Andrews, Mary Raymond, *The Perfect Tribute.* New York, Charles Scribner's Sons, 1906.

Angle, Paul M., *Here I Have Lived: Lincoln's Springfield.* New Brunswick, Rutgers University Press, 1950.

Basler, Roy P., *The Lincoln Legend*. Octagon Books, 1969.

Donald, David, *Lincoln Reconsidered: Essays on the Civil War Era*. New York, Random House, Inc.

Thomas, Benjamin P., *Lincoln's New Salem*. New York, Alfred A. Knopf, Inc., 1954.

Trueblood, Elton, *Abraham Lincoln: Theologian of American Anguish*. New York, Harper & Row Publishers, Inc., 1973.

Williams, T. Harry, *Lincoln and His Generals*. New York, Knopf, Inc., 1952.

Wolf, William J., *Lincoln's Religion*. Philadelphia, United Church Press, 1970.

About the Author

During his thirty years as a history teacher for young people, William H. Armstrong has written extensively in the field of education. In 1961 he won *The Independent School Bulletin* award for the best article of the year. In 1963 he won the National School Bell award for "Distinguished Interpretation in the Field of Education" for his contributions to a series of articles in *Better Homes and Gardens* magazine.

His *Study Is Hard Work*, published in 1956 and revised in 1967, is a widely used textbook of study habits and motivation. He is also the author of *87 Ways to Help Your Child in School,* published in 1961, and *Tools of Thinking*, published in 1969.

Mr. Armstrong's novel *Sounder*, published in 1970, won the distinguished Newbery Award, the Mark Twain Award, and the Nene Award. He is also the author of several other novels, including *The MacLeod Place*, a history of the ancient world, and a biography of Grandma Moses.

William H. Armstrong lives in a house he designed and built for his family overlooking the Housatonic River in Connecticut.